T0271145

On Central Banking

In these six lectures given at the Norwegian Royal Academy of Science and Letters, Jan Fredrik Qvigstad draws on his deep experience at Norges Bank to outline key principles on which to base central bank policy. The first two lectures (about keeping promises and transparency) emphasize the importance of credibility and ensuring accountability. Lectures 3–6 can be viewed as applying these key principles to specific issues (making good decisions, managing wealth, learning from history, and institutions). The lectures do not break new ground – indeed, Qvigstad nicely illustrates how these principles have been articulated in literature, history, and politics. Rather, the lectures emphasize the lessons to be learned by applying these principles to central banking history with primary reference to the case of Norway, such as managing Norway's sovereign wealth fund and designing institutions that will produce good policy outcomes.

Jan Fredrik Qvigstad (born 1949) was Deputy Governor and Deputy Chair of the Executive Board of Norges Bank 2008–2014. From 1997 he was Chief Economist of Norges Bank. He is now the Executive Director, General Staff, at Norges Bank with the responsibility for the bank's economic history project.

Advance Praise for *On Central Banking*

"Jan Fredrik Qvigstad's *On Central Banking* revives European essay writing in the tradition of Michel de Montaigne or David Hume. The lectures, collected in this volume, reflect a very well-read author and a lifetime of experience. At the same time, they read like letters from a wise friend who says: 'I have tried it and it worked well for me.'"

Vitor Gaspar, Director of Fiscal Affairs Department, International Monetary Fund

"*On Central Banking* is a highly entertaining and insightful collection of lectures that will appeal not only to those interested in central banks, but also to a wide audience of regulators, politicians, church leaders, and others. Drawing on history, academic theories from various subjects, and the author's own experiences, this is a fascinating discussion of what makes for effective and legitimate institutions."

Anne Sibert, Professor of Economics, Birkbeck, University of London

STUDIES IN MACROECONOMIC HISTORY

Series Editor: Michael D. Bordo, *Rutgers University*

Editors:

Owen F. Humpage, *Federal Reserve Bank of Cleveland*
Christopher M. Meissner, *University of California, Davis*
Kris James Mitchener, *Santa Clara University*
David C. Wheelock, *Federal Reserve Bank of St. Louis*

The titles in this series investigate themes of interest to economists and economic historians in the rapidly developing field of macroeconomic history. The four areas covered include the application of monetary and finance theory, international economics, and quantitative methods to historical problems; the historical application of growth and development theory and theories of business fluctuations; the history of domestic and international monetary, financial, and other macroeconomic institutions; and the history of international monetary and financial systems. The series amalgamates the former Cambridge University Press series *Studies in Monetary and Financial History* and *Studies in Quantitative Economic History*.

Other books in the series:

Continued after Index

On Central Banking

Jan Fredrik Qvigstad

CAMBRIDGE
UNIVERSITY PRESS

CAMBRIDGE
UNIVERSITY PRESS

University Printing House, Cambridge CB2 8BS, United Kingdom

One Liberty Plaza, 20th Floor, New York, NY 10006, USA

477 Williamstown Road, Port Melbourne, VIC 3207, Australia

4843/24, 2nd Floor, Ansari Road, Daryaganj, Delhi - 110002, India

79 Anson Road, #06-04/06, Singapore 079906

Cambridge University Press is part of the University of Cambridge.

It furthers the University's mission by disseminating knowledge in the pursuit of education, learning and research at the highest international levels of excellence.

www.cambridge.org
Information on this title: www.cambridge.org/9781107150973

First published 2016

A catalogue record for this publication is available from the British Library

Library of Congress Cataloging in Publication data
Names: Qvigstad, Jan Fredrik, author.
Title: On central banking / Jan Fredrik Qvigstad.
Description: 1 Edition. | New York : Cambridge University Press, 2016. |
Series: Studies in macroeconomic history | "Contains six lectures given at the Norwegian Academy of Science and Letters." | Includes bibliographical references and index.
Identifiers: LCCN 2016000902 | ISBN 9781107150973 (Hardback)
Subjects: LCSH: Banks and banking, Central. | Transparency in international agencies. | Monetary policy. | Trust.
Classification: LCC HG1811 .Q85 2016 | DDC 332.1/1–dc23 LC record available at http://lccn.loc.gov/2016000902

ISBN 978-1-107-15097-3 Hardback
ISBN 978-1-316-60548-6 Paperback

To my wife Nina and children Maria Céline
and Lars Fredrik

Contents

Foreword

Michael D. Bordo

I first met Jan F. Qvigstad in the spring of 2007 when he and Øyvind Eitrheim came to see me at King's College, Cambridge, when I was on sabbatical, to discuss the plans for the Norges Bank's bicentenary celebration. Jan is a very impressive central bank deputy governor who is not only a very able technical monetary economist but also a polymath – he is a scholar of the arts, the sciences, and the humanities.

Jan has spent much of his career at Norges Bank with some excursions to the academic world. He worked his way up the ladder to become Deputy Governor and Vice-Chairman of the Executive Board of the Norwegian Sovereign Wealth Fund. As an economist he has written a number of important policy papers, including one in 2006, "When Does an Interest Rate Path 'Look Good'? Criteria for an Appropriate Future Interest Rate Path" which has led to what Carl Walsh, a leading scholar of central banking, has recently dubbed

the Qvigstad Rule, a useful rule of thumb for inflation targeting central banks to assess monetary policy.... It has the advantage of focusing on things we care about – inflation and real activity – rather than the setting of the policy instrument.... If inflation is above target the output gap should be negative and vice versa. If inflation is above target and the output gap is also positive, then policy is too loose; if inflation is below target and the output gap is negative, policy is too tight. (Walsh 2014)[1]

Most important and most interesting are the six annual lectures Jan gave at the Norwegian Academy of Science and Letters from 2008 to 2013. The lectures are lessons or homilies for how to be a good central banker. All the lectures are grounded in the history of Norges Bank and the history of central banking in general. The six lectures are intertwined and then summarized in his most recent lecture, "On Institutions."

---

[1] Carl E. Walsh (2014), "Monetary policy objectives and central bank trade-offs under flexible inflation targeting," Keynote address, 16th Annual Inflation Targeting Seminar, Banco Central do Brazil, May 15–16, 2014.

Lecture 1: On Keeping Promises

To establish credibility central banks have to keep their promises. Promises are hard to keep because future temptations come along to break them. For a central bank the promise to maintain the value of money, that is, to maintain price stability, can be hard to keep in the face of political pressure to reduce unemployment or stimulate output during a recession. To keep its promises the central bank needs to follow the example of Ulysses and be bound to the mast to resist the sirens' songs. This fundamental idea was put forth by the philosopher Jon Elster (1979)[2] and by the economists Thomas Schelling (1960)[3] and Finn Kydland and Edward Prescott (1977).[4] Being tied to the mast prevents short-run objectives from dominating long-run objectives. To follow through on its key mandate to maintain price stability the central bank needs to be backed up by the government.

[2] Jon Elster (1979), *Ulysses and the Sirens: Studies in Rationality and Irrationality*, Cambridge University Press.

[3] Thomas C. Schelling (1960), *The Strategy of Conflict*, Cambridge, Mass.: Harvard University Press.

[4] Finn E. Kydland and Edward C. Prescott (1977), "Rules Rather Than Discretion: The Inconsistency of Optimal Plans," *Journal of Political Economy*, Vol. 85, No. 3, pp. 473–491.

Foreword

The history of monetary policy is rife with precommitment mechanisms that didn't work. The specie standard that prevailed through much of recorded history made keeping promises easy to monitor. Coin defined as a fixed weight of gold or silver could be relatively easy to ascertain by the market. Still, in times of turbulence, monarchs were tempted to debase the coinage to gain seignorage revenue. The best known culprits were the kings of France and Burgundy in the fifteenth century and Henry VIII of England in the sixteenth century. With the advent of bank notes and government chartered banks of issue, keeping promises meant maintaining the convertibility of paper notes into specie at a fixed exchange rate – the specie standard rule. New technology made the temptation to overissue easier. The shift to a fiat money standard in the twentieth century increased opportunities for breaking promises because of the loss of the specie nominal anchor. It took until the 1980s for credibility to maintain low inflation to be restored.

Within this general framework of world monetary history Jan examines the record of Norges Bank with keeping promises. When Norges Bank was founded in 1816 the key problem it faced was the legacy of high inflation after the Napoleonic wars. The bank introduced a currency convertible into silver called the speciedaler. A big problem was that Norges Bank did not have large enough silver reserves to fully back the new currency. It took twenty years to restore full convertibility but credibility was attained by "the long promise" to steadily contract the money supply until convertibility could be achieved. From the 1840s until World War I Norway, like other advanced countries, followed the specie standard rule, leading to an era of price stability and good macroeconomic performance. The good pattern broke with World War I and a return to high inflation and macro instability. After the war, Governor Nicolai Rygg followed the specie standard rule and engineered a serious deflation accompanied by recession to achieve convertibility at the prewar parity. A backlash triggered by the real costs of his "par" policy carried through much of the rest of the twentieth century. After World War II, Norway eagerly adopted Keynesian aggregate demand management and went further into indicative planning and credit allocation (like other European countries). These policies eventually led to rising inflation, sluggish growth, and frequent devaluations, culminating in a period of unstable money in the 1970s. The return to keeping promises came in 1986 with the decision by the government to have a mandate for low inflation and, eventually, give the Norges Bank the independence to implement it via inflation targeting.

Lecture 2: On Transparency

Central bank transparency and accountability is today viewed as key to maintaining credibility for low inflation. In earlier times central banks acted in secrecy and good central bank governors learned to be as cryptic as possible; for example, the maestro Alan Greenspan was impossible to understand. Today central banks try to be as open and transparent as possible so they can achieve their objectives of low inflation and low inflation expectations. Indeed, transparency is a way to manage inflation expectations. In this lecture Jan complements the previous lecture on keeping promises by narrating how central bank transparency evolved through the ages.

Under the specie standard, when the key objective was to maintain the fixed price of gold, it was easy to observe the central bank's gold reserves. This carried forward to the post–World War II realm of fixed exchange rates. With respect to lender of last resort policy, Walter Bagehot's strictures told central banks to announce their policy clearly and in advance. The shift to managed fiat standards and central banks providing stabilization policy became associated with central bank secrecy in revealing their interest rate policies in the belief that unexpected policy could influence the markets. This was jettisoned in the 1970s and 1980s with the rational expectations revolution and the belief in central bank credibility as a way to anchor inflation expectations. Central bank transparency became the norm worldwide.

Jan surveys Norges Bank's experience. Like other countries it followed the specie standard and later fixed exchange rates with a modicum of transparency except at times when devaluation seemed imminent. With the shift to the emphasis on low and stable inflation and credibility (the keeping of promises), it became important to become transparent and to communicate the central bank's intentions. Norges Bank has the best record in the world in transmitting its intentions, its forecasts, and the models it uses. Norges Bank follows the collegial approach, in contrast to the individualistic approach of the Bank of England and the Riksbank. This has a bearing on how the minutes can be written and published. Detailed minutes with a collegial approach is difficult because the board members would be reluctant to let their views be recorded.

Lecture 3: On Making Good Decisions

Norges Bank as an independent central bank has been delegated the mandate to provide price stability. It targets inflation, varies the policy rate to hit its inflation target, and has to make decisions on when to raise and lower the rate. Decisions matter a lot because they affect the public's view of the competence and quality of the central bank. The problem with decision making is that we live in an uncertain world. Jan discusses how decisions were made in Norges Bank's history. Two important episodes stand out: when the United Kingdom devalued the pound in 1931 and when it devalued in 1949. Norway, as a small open economy with close trade ties to the United Kingdom, to avoid being at a competitive disadvantage, followed the United Kingdom's lead in 1931. As a consequence, like the other countries that followed the United Kingdom's lead, it recovered quickly from the Great Depression. In 1949 it followed the same rule of thumb as in 1931 and devalued by the same amount as the United Kingdom. This time, the outcome was different: Norway suffered high inflation. The difference between the two episodes was that in the earlier one there was substantial economic slack while in the later episode there was excess aggregate demand. The prevailing economic conditions were not closely considered by the monetary authorities.

Jan describes how today the Norges Bank's Executive Committee makes decisions using the expertise of its research department and its collegiality-based committee system. However, he points out that Norges Bank's approach runs the risk of groupthink, which is why most of its members come from outside the bank. He argues that Norges Bank's decision making is sharpened by the clarity of its mandate to maintain an inflation target of 2.5 percent over a longer period. This allows it the flexibility in the short term to deal with shocks to the real economy while always maintaining its long-term goal. Good decision making is tied in closely with transparency and with keeping promises. Transparency is a precondition for accountability, which focuses the minds of policy makers to make the best decisions possible.

Lecture 4: On Managing Wealth

As Deputy Governor Jan F. Qvigstad was the vice-chairman of the Executive Board of the Norwegian Sovereign Wealth Fund (SWF) called "Government Pension Fund Global" (which is managent by Norges Bank Investment Management (NBIM)). In Lecture 4 he describes how he perceives his mandate. Norway has so far avoided the Dutch Disease where a sudden increase in oil revenues can lead to the misallocation of resources toward the oil-producing sector and to eventual impoverishment. The Norwegian SWF has invested the oil revenues and a fiscal policy rule secures that only the returns on its previous investments are spent.

Jan explains how the fund allocates its asset purchases between bonds and primarily foreign equities and how it selects the companies it invests in, paying close attention to avoiding investing in companies "violating fundamental humanitarian principles." As one of the largest SWFs, Government Pension Fund Global accounts for 1 percent of global equities, yet it has avoided exerting undue influences in its member countries. Norway is fortunate to have its oil resources and such a well-managed SWF.

Lecture 5: On Learning from History

Qvigstad employs Thomas Kuhn's (1962)[5] concept of paradigm shifts to analyze the theoretical backgrounds to policy making in history. He starts with the classical approach to fiscal policy – to always maintain balanced budgets. This was the view of the Norwegian Director General at the Ministry of Finance, Mr. Nissen, right after World War II. This approach was quickly eclipsed by the Keynesian paradigm, which posited active budget management to stabilize the economy and to allocate resources. The Keynesian/Frischian vision dominated

[5] Thomas Kuhn (1962), *The Structure of Scientific Revolutions*, University of Chicago Press.

Norwegian macro policy making from the 1940s to the 1970s. By the 1970s a disconnect between the reality of large deficits, high inflation, and weak economic performance led to a new Kuhnian paradigm shift toward the Lucasian rational expectations approach, which emphasized the role of free markets rather than government intervention, and monetary and fiscal policy based on transparent rule-like behavior. This produced the Great Moderation, which lasted until the financial crisis of 2007–2008. Time will tell if the paradigm will last.

Jan argues that there is learning from history but that caution needs to be exercised before discarding the old paradigm. According to him, the simple balanced budget rule of Director General Nissen in 1945 would have helped the Europeans avoid the ravages of the recent Eurozone crisis while Keynesian policies of spending in recessions and saving in the boom could also have been helpful.

His desired prescription is to follow simple rules such as his "Rule of Four" (Llewellyn and Qvigstad 2012, pp. 31–44).[6] When the current account deficit exceeds 4 percent of GDP, inflation exceeds 4 percent, unemployment exceeds 4 percent, and bank lending exceeds 4 times

[6] See John Llewellyn and Jan F. Qvigstad (2012), "The 'Rule of Four,'" *The Business Economist*, Vol. 43, No. 1.

the GDP, the economy is heading for trouble. Simple rules in an environment of confidence in policy making will carry the policy maker far but, according to Jan, there is no Faustian magic wand and real economic problems need real economic adjustments.

Lecture 6: On Institutions

Qvigstad uses Acemoglu and Robinson's (2012)[7] distinction between inclusive and extractive institutions as a backdrop to describing how the Norges Bank evolved as a "good institution." Inclusive institutions exist to serve the people, while extractive institutions foster rent seeking. After the industrial revolution Norway shifted from the "old society," based on the institutions of the family and the village, to a modern economy. Upon independence in 1814 sound institutions were established with the Constitution, the Supreme Court, the Norges Bank, and the public school system.

The Glorious Revolution in England in 1688 set that country on the path of sound institutions, which backstopped the development of markets and the division of labor. The concept of sound institutions applies to the

---

[7] D. Acemoglu and J. Robinson (2012), *Why Nations Fail: The Origins of Power, Prosperity and Poverty*, New York: Crown Publishers.

monetary system, which has evolved from specie to the present fiat system. Institutional developments that prevented debasement and the overissue of paper money preserved the functions of money as a store of value, unit of account, and medium of exchange – key ingredients to provide grounding for economic development.

Jan describes the key defining moments in the Norges Bank's path to becoming a cutting-edge, credible central bank. The defining moments mentioned in earlier lectures were the speciedaler and "the long promise," which led to the transition between the Napoleonic war inflation to the stable money of the specie standard; the resumption of gold convertibility called "par" policy in the 1920s under Nicolai Rygg, which damaged the reputation of the Norges Bank and led it (as was the case in other countries) to lose its independence to the fisc; the Keynesian/Frischian interlude from the 1940s to the 1970s that ended with ten devaluations and high inflation; and the policy shift in 1986 to the Norges Bank regaining its independence, adopting a mandate for price stability and adopting inflation targeting in 2001. Jan calls the period 1986–2001 "the long return." So the 200-year history of Norges Bank starts with "the long promise" (from monetary chaos to price stability) and ends with "the long return" (to price stability).

Qvigstad concludes his lecture series with four key principles for a sound central bank: (1) it must keep its promises, (2) it must make good decisions, (3) it must be transparent, and (4) it must learn from history. The Norges Bank under the guidance of Jan F. Qvigstad and his predecessors is certainly a good example of these principles.

The Lecture Not Held: On Mediocrity

After each of lectures in the Norwegian Academy of Science and Letters there was a general discussion. In his closing remark, Jan used to announce the theme for next year's lecture. The sixth lecture was the last one, but even so Jan said that if there should have been a next one, the theme would have been "On Mediocrity." The reasoning he gave was the following: Institutions are often measured in terms of their role and credibility. It is not easy to measure credibility, but it is done. Norway scores high on such confidence measures. Some assessments for Russia show that the level of output would have been 70 percent higher if the country's confidence measure had been as high as was the measure for Sweden. Confidence is important for economic prosperity. Individual institutions are also measured. But the scores are not static. They may rise or fall. Norges Bank is today among the highest ranking in such surveys.

But Norges Bank must not rest on its laurels. A central bank must be competent if it is to maintain its credibility. As a starting point the central bank is somewhat handicapped in this respect.

There are two main reasons for this: Norges Bank is a monopolistic institution. It is the only central bank in the country. There is no other benchmark within the nation. Second, the institution has at its disposal a potentially enormous budget. It prints its money. Printing a 1,000 krone note costs half a krone and the bank can sell the printed note for 1,000 kroner. The potential financial leeway is substantial. An undertaking needs a good-sized budget, but not one that is too big! One may easily become self-satisfied. So, even if Norges Bank has a high ranking in terms of reputation and confidence, it can quickly slip into a mood of self-satisfaction and then mediocrity. It is up to Norges Bank to put into place the mechanisms to prevent this from occurring. The central bank must tie itself to the mast.

What can a central bank do? The first element is transparency. It must expose itself to criticism. The second element is an international dimension. It must be part of the international community of central banks and academia to provide a basis for comparison. Governor Erik Brofoss was central bank governor from 1954 to 1970 and was perhaps more concerned with questions outside the realm of central banking. But he was the one who laid part of the foundation for the "long return" – perhaps without knowing the scope of what was to follow or the eventual outcome. Brofoss was intent on sending young economists at the bank out into the world to learn. When they came back, they had learned that another world was possible, benefiting from input about what central banks should be doing and how monetary and credit policy should be conducted. Today, there is a research unit at the bank. Its research output is useful, but a drop in the ocean in relation to the totality of the research produced in the world. But the research unit is important to keep the central bank on its toes. It is the bank's bridge to the academic world within and outside Norway. Internationally recognized researchers visit the bank every week and inform it of the most recent research developments and challenges for its perceptions and thinking. The very presence of internal researchers with specialized competence in the area of central banking keeps other staff on the ball. The research unit keeps the bank as an institution from isolating itself, from becoming introverted and self-satisfied. The third element is a good interplay between the bank's executive bodies and staff. Most of the literature on "making good decisions" is concerned with the composition of the board (external vs. internal and experts vs. general

Foreword

competence) and their decision-making bodies (collegial vs. individualistic committees). Not least, it is important that the board use its staff competence effectively. If an institution such as Norges Bank slowly slides into mediocrity, it will not be discovered until it is too late

From reading Jan's lectures you realize that he is not just another boring central bank economist who looks at his shoes, but a polymath who is interested in everything. In his lectures, especially in the footnotes, he quotes from and cites, in addition to economics books and articles, history, philosophy, psychology, law, sociology, poetry, and drama. Jan also has his whimsical side, with occasional references to Harry Potter. The Norges Bank is fortunate to have him on board, as is the fraternity of central bankers.

Preface

"Money makes the world go around," they sing in the musical *Cabaret*. The musical is dark and melancholic. The song's message is that money makes the world go around; not love, not having children and grandchildren – just money.

As economists we think otherwise. We think that money is not an end in itself. Money is the oil in the machinery that helps the economy to function. We think of money as the unit of account, just like distance is a unit of measurement. It would be meaningless to answer the question "How far is it?" with 110. One must add the unit of measurement, "yards" or "meters." Money is useful as means of payment so that one can avoid returning to a barter economy. Money is also a store of value, creating a time gap between earning and spending to allow borrowing in the meantime, which facilitates investment. Money, however, only functions in an efficient way if there is trust and confidence. In early times money circulated in the form of coins, with a promised content of silver, copper, or gold. It was tempting to debase the coins and reduce or replace some of the silver with less valuable metals. When paper money came into use in the form of banknotes, it was tempting to produce too many of them, until their value depreciated and they could no longer be exchanged into the promised silver or gold content. Since the mid-nineteenth century, money has mainly been in the form of bank deposits. Trust is still critical, not least our trust in banks. As the economy develops and grows more sophisticated, so does money. In a modern society, it is inconceivable for the world to go around without money. Modern societies have delegated the task of safekeeping money to central banks.

On Central Banking contains six lectures given at the Norwegian Academy of Science and Letters. The lectures analyze different aspects of central banking but the questions raised could also be relevant for other institutions in society. The key words are trust and confidence. A prerequisite for trust and confidence is keeping promises. But in a modern open society, the central bank must do more. It must also be transparent and explain its functions and decisions to the public. Yet there is no point

in keeping promises and being transparent if the decisions are bad. How does one make good decisions? Central banks are institutions that have a long memory. At
the same time a central bank must be light on its feet
when new challenges arise. So what truths are delimited
to period and what truths are eternal? Central banks
must be able to learn from history. But again, a central
bank that keeps its promises, is transparent, makes good
decisions, has a long institutional memory but is still able
to learn from history, and is able to differentiate between
ephemeral truths and eternal truths may still be an inadequate central bank. It must be a useful institution that
does not forget that it serves the public. A public servant
must never forget the importance of serving the public.
The same applies to the central bank. But a central bank is
the only such institution in a country, and it prints its
own money. It can quickly slip into a mood of complacency and then mediocrity. It is up to central banks to
put into place the mechanisms to prevent this from
occurring. The central bank must tie itself to the mast.
Transparency, engagement in the international community, and an efficient and highly qualified staff are
important safeguards against mediocrity.

The lectures on central banking were given at the
Royal Academy of Science and Letters. The seminars
were designed to promote debate on key social and

economic issues, particularly in areas of importance to the central bank, but the themes are far-reaching and lend themselves to discussion across disciplines and institutions such as the Supreme Court; the collegium of bishops of the Norwegian Church; the Parliamentary Ombudsman; Higher Prosecution Authorities; professors of philosophy, history, physics; and the like. The lectures were intended to reach out to a wider academic group than economists only.

There is a personal history behind the title of my book, *On Central Banking*, and the lectures "On Keeping Promises," "On Transparency," and so on.

In the early 1970s I was the research assistant to Professor Trygve Haavelmo (Nobel Prize in Economics, 1989). Our exams at the university lasted eight hours. When Haavelmo gave the exams, they were usually titled "On the labor market," "On inflation," and so on. The exam candidates who wrote all they knew about the labor market or inflation theory for eight hours failed the exam. Haavelmo believed that by posing the right question, you can solve the problem. The question had to be sufficiently precise so that it could be subject to a meaningful analysis. A complex group of problems can generally be divided into many questions. The right approach was therefore to enumerate a list of questions and analyze each of them. This is what I learned from

Haavelmo, and also what I have attempted to do in these six lectures.

Haavelmo and I became quite good friends. He had a cabin up in the mountains not far from where my family had a cabin. The mountains were also the home to wild reindeer and trout. Haavelmo was an angler. When hiking there in the early 1990s, I met a local reindeer hunter. I asked him if he knew Haavelmo. He assured me that he did. "Haavelmo is a mountain man," he said. I asked him if he knew that Haavelmo was a famous professor. He did not know that. He thought he lived up there because he was always fishing.

— ✜ CHAPTER ONE ✜ —

On Keeping Promises

Why Is Keeping Promises So Difficult?

This house, which now belongs to the Norwegian Academy of Science and Letters, was built by Hans Rasmus Astrup in 1886–1887.[*] Astrup was an entrepreneur. At the age of 20, he left Norway for Barcelona on a ship laden with a cargo of dried cod. He gradually built up a large trading business and later became an industrialist, not unlike businessmen of our own era.[1]

---

[*] I would like to thank Ragna Alstadheim for her valuable assistance in preparing this lecture. I would also like to thank Helle Snellingen for her contribution to the translation of the Norwegian text into English.

[1] See Reidar Sevåg (1967), *Statsråd H. R. Astrup*, Oslo: Dreyer.

For innovators and the business sector, a stable operating environment has always been important, providing a foundation for adaptation, economic growth, and social progress. A stable value of money is also a component of this foundation.

We were taught as children to keep our promises. If we made a promise, we had to make good on it. But we were also taught that we should not promise too much. If we do not keep our word, others lose confidence in us and our credibility takes a toll. In recent months, we have witnessed that this is of particular importance for the financial system. A proximate example is the situation in our neighboring country Iceland.

The value of confidence and credibility has been the subject of extensive analysis in many fields, including jurisprudence and the social sciences. And the conclusion is clear – progress can be achieved if promises are kept.

If keeping promises is clearly beneficial, why is it then so difficult? The expressions "empty promises" and "empty threats" reflect the temptation to renege. The social scientist and philosopher Jon Elster writes in his book *Ulysses and the Sirens*[2] about weakness of will, shifting preferences over time, and the complexities of

[2] See Jon Elster (1979), *Ulysses and the Sirens: Studies in Rationality and Irrationality*, Cambridge University Press.

human nature. This is familiar ground. As early as 1960, the economist Thomas Schelling[3] discussed similar issues in analyses for which he was awarded the Nobel Prize in economics. According to Schelling, a credible threat can be difficult to establish when realizing the threat involves costs for all the parties involved. A promise or a threat will be more credible if the promisor lets himself be bound to the mast.

Two other economists carried out groundbreaking work when they applied Schelling's analysis to economic issues. In 1977, Finn Kydland from Norway and Edward Prescott[4] from the United States wrote an article showing that authorities who attempt to follow an optimal economic policy plan may have strong incentives to depart from the same plan at a later time.[5] This applies even if no news has emerged to indicate that the plan should be changed. Kydland and Prescott were later awarded the Nobel Prize in Economics for their work.

---

[3] Thomas C. Schelling (1960), *The Strategy of Conflict*, Cambridge, Mass.: Harvard University Press.

[4] Finn E. Kydland and Edward C. Prescott (1977), "Rules Rather Than Discretion: The Inconsistency of Optimal Plans," *Journal of Political Economy*, Vol. 85, No. 3, pp. 473–491.

[5] In macroeconomics, this dilemma is called the time inconsistency problem.

On Central Banking

There is a common denominator between Elster, Schelling, Kydland, and Prescott: keeping a promise is difficult, because reneging on a promise will often be the tempting or rational choice in the short term. If loss of credibility is taken into account, the best solution in the long term will nonetheless often be to keep your word.

A key issue is how we can establish mechanisms that also safeguard long-term objectives in the short term. Jon Elster suggested the metaphor of "binding oneself to the mast." We all know the myth of Ulysses and the sirens, referred to in Elster's work. Ulysses wanted to hear the song of the sirens, but he knew that he and his crew would then come under the sirens' spell, bringing their voyage to an end. He therefore ordered the crew to bind him to the mast, but before they did so, he filled their ears with wax. This prevented him from steering the ship toward the sirens himself, and the crew was prevented from hearing him when he would later succumb to temptation and order the ship to be steered toward the sirens' island. The story cannot be directly transferred to economic management, but the concept of "tying oneself to the mast" is used to describe mechanisms that prevent short-term objectives from taking precedence over long-term objectives. Precluding the possibility of breaking a promise makes the promise more credible. Ensuring accountability for promises made through reporting and review can be a mechanism that binds us to the mast.

A central bank's most important task is to ensure a stable value of money. The value of money relies on responsible economic policies. For a central bank to be able to keep its promise and deliver a stable value of money, it must have the backing of the political authorities. Otherwise, the central bank will not be able to keep its promise.

In the long term, the instruments available to the central bank allow it to deliver only the promise of a stable value of money. Earlier, this promise was kept by regulating the amount of money issued. Today, the instrument is the interest rate. The central bank cannot steer real wages, the labor supply, employment, or the level of unemployment in the long term. But it can contribute to curbing short-term cyclical fluctuations if price stability is firmly anchored.

Throughout history, central banks have attempted to bind themselves to the mast in different ways. In the following, I will discuss the temptations facing issuers of notes and coins, the binding mechanisms that have been tested, and the potential gains for society of a central bank that keeps its promises.

A King's Word Is Worth a Throne – But Sometimes Not a Krone

It has always been tempting for issuers of money to exploit this privilege. It costs less to produce a coin or a banknote than the value printed on it. The added value accruing to the issuer is called seignorage.

Overissuance of notes and coins leads to inflation and a fall in the value of money, and holders of money pay a so-called inflation tax. A sharp fall or strong rise in the value of money also impairs the functioning of the economy because it becomes more difficult to keep track of changes in the price of one good relative to another. It is important that changes in relative prices are easy for both consumers and producers to observe. Otherwise, the function of prices as conveyors of information for consumption, production, and investment decisions will be impaired. The economy will operate less efficiently, resulting in lower growth and welfare.

In the earliest monetary systems, the value of money corresponded to the metal value of the coin. Measured in metal, the value of money was inevitably stable. This system was not as dependent on confidence since the metal content of the coin could in principle be verified at every transaction.

On Keeping Promises

Those in power nevertheless managed to exploit the system. Roman emperors were in the habit of financing their wars by reducing the precious metal content of their coins. This resulted in higher seignorage revenues from each coin issued. For a period, these revenues were sufficient to finance an army, a long war, or several monuments. This is the number one temptation facing money issuers.

Henry VIII of England was one of the most renowned exponents of this kind of behavior[6]. In the 1500s, he reduced the silver content in coins to one third of the original to finance wars against France and his own expensive lifestyle.

In addition to coins, a system gradually developed involving paper money. Banknotes were a receipt for a money issuer's claims on silver or gold. Instead of using coins as a means of payment, the receipt was used. This was more practical, but with the introduction of banknotes the authorities also introduced a new promise. They promised the bearer that they would redeem the nominal value of the notes in silver or gold. The value of the notes was entirely dependent on confidence in the issuer's promise. The authorities' ability to fulfill their

[6] Glyn Davies (2002), *A History of Money from Ancient Times to the Present Day*, University of Wales Press, p. 200.

promises depended on government finances. Brutal tax collectors, a well-filled treasury, and peace with neighboring countries inspired confidence in the authorities' ability to redeem the notes in a precious metal then or at some time in the future.

The authorities often granted a monopoly on banknote issuance to an institution they controlled. This was no coincidence in view of the seignorage revenues generated by printing money. This method of raising seignorage is temptation number two: the authorities borrow money from the issuing bank and the issuing bank provides the loan by printing banknotes. This was particularly common in times of war. It can be difficult to raise taxes or borrow directly from the public to fund an unpopular war. Naturally, a regime at war will be more interested in winning the war than in the long-term economic costs. Who cares about high inflation and debt repayment if surviving as a regime is at stake?

Confidence – and the lack of it – had important consequences for England and France during the Napoleonic Wars. England was able to finance these wars more easily than France. The English government could draw on several funding sources. They raised taxes, but could also borrow, partly from the public and partly from the central bank. They had previously demonstrated that they stood by their commitments, and were therefore granted loans. The French government, on the other hand, had lost its creditworthiness after Louis XVI was sent to the guillotine. The only source of funding that remained was taxation, eliminating the option of spreading war expenditure over time.[7]

Norway's history also illustrates the costs of inflation and a loss of confidence. Soaring inflation in Norway during and after the Napoleonic Wars impaired the functioning of the payment system. The function of money as a unit of measurement was also undermined. An example of this is described in the local history books for the coastal districts of Karlsøy and Helgøy in Troms, northern Norway. At that time, accounts were sometimes kept in silver, or in goods such as cod liver oil, pollock, or flour[8].

Inflation also resulted in the transfer of assets from creditors to debtors: the real value of the fishermen's debt to merchants in Bergen decreased. This marked a historic shift. The fishermen were of course happy to see their

---

[7] Michael D. Bordo and Eugene N. White (1990), "British and French Finance during the Napoleonic Wars," NBER Working Paper No. 3517, also published in Michael D. Bordo and Forrest Capie (Eds.) (1993), *Monetary Regimes in Transition*, Cambridge University Press.

[8] Håvard Dahl Bratrein (1989–1994), *Karlsøy og Helgøy bygdebok*, Karlsøy kommune, http://karlsoy.com/bygdebok/.

debt diminish. Creditors, however, lost money, which probably did not increase confidence and a willingness to lend the next time someone needed a loan.

The Promise of a Stable Value of Money against Gold and Silver

I have given examples of how easily monarchs succumbed to the temptation of an apparently free lunch by exploiting opportunities for raising seignorage revenues. In times of political instability, they sometimes had no choice. But eventually, the authorities learned that the costs were high. The public pays an inflation tax, the monetary system is impaired, and economic growth slows.

The economic progress experienced by Norway and other countries in the second half of the 1800s was founded on more than a thousand years of money and credit history. The authorities probably knew that a credible promise of a stable value of money measured in metal was one of the cornerstones of the success experienced by towns in northern Italy during the Renaissance and in seventeenth-century Netherlands. They knew that confidence in the promise of a stable value of money could be maintained by relinquishing seignorage and limiting the issuance of money. The opposite was equally true. Kåre Lunden, for example, writes that "after 1387, no coins were minted in Norway for a hundred years." According to Lunden, the deep crisis in the Norwegian economy between 1350 and 1500 was due not only to the Black Death but also to the absence of a monetary system.[9]

Stability in the value of money eliminated uncertainty and doubt among potential investors. Long-term planning became easier. Providers of credit could be reasonably certain that their investment would not be inflated away. They did not have to move their wealth into property or other fixed investments in order to preserve it. The willingness to save and accumulate wealth increased.

History had taught the authorities the value of price stability, and the commitment mechanism was a monetary system linked to silver or gold. The whims of French kings were replaced by parliaments that were accountable to the people. It is no coincidence that the name of the most prominent great power's monetary unit – the pound – reflected a measure of weight: the value of a pound of silver.[10]

---

[9] Kåre Lunden (2008), "Kriser og pengestell," *Klassekampen,* 11 November, pp. 12–13.

[10] David Sinclair (2000), *The Pound: A Biography,* London: Century.

On Central Banking

Credibility hinged on orderly government finances and a stable political situation, which contained seignorage temptations and in turn strengthened public confidence in the value of money. These conditions need to be in place to enable a central bank to keep its promise!

When Norges Bank was established in 1816, credibility was ensured by establishing a tax-financed silver fund. A par value against silver for the new paper money – the speciedaler – was announced. However, the market value of the speciedaler was considerably below par value – the authorities in our young country were in a difficult financial situation and had not yet established confidence. It was not until 1822 that the authorities were able to establish a more orderly system when the Storting adopted a long-term strategy whereby the silver value of the speciedaler would gradually increase to par value.[11] This goal was reached in 1842, twenty years later, bearing witness to long-termism and persistence in policy implementation.

[11] Øyvind Eitrheim (2005) in Øyvind Eitrheim and Jan F. Qvigstad (Eds.) (2005), "Tilbakeblikk på norsk pengehistorie. Konferanse 7. juni 2005 på Bogstad gård (Norwegian monetary history in retrospect. Conference, 7 June 2005, Oslo)," *Occasional Papers* No. 37, Norges Bank.

And persistence was rewarded. The rest of the 1800s and the period until World War I were generally characterized by price stability and strong growth in the Norwegian economy, even though there were also periods of weaker growth.[12] Toward the end of this period, confidence provided Norges Bank with the scope to adjust the interest rate to the domestic economic situation rather than solely in relation to the gold standard.[13,14]

The Era of Broken Promises

The interwar years proved to be highly turbulent, both in Norway and abroad. In 1921, for example, per capita GDP in Norway fell by 11 percent. The structure of the

[12] See, for example, Fritz Hodne and Ola Honningdal Grytten (2000), *Norsk økonomi i det 19. århundre* (*The Norwegian economy in the 19th century*), Bergen: Fagbokforlaget.

[13] In Norway, the silver standard was replaced by the gold standard on 1 January 1874. See annex by Ragna Alstadheim in "Valutakursregimer – historiske erfaringer og fremtidige utfordringer (Exchange rate regimes – historical experience and future challenges)," by Jan F. Qvigstad and Arent Skjæveland (1994) in *Stabilitet og langsiktighet: Festskrift til Hermod Skånland* (*Stability and a longtermism: Festschrift for Hermod Skånland*), Oslo: Aschehoug.

[14] Lars Fredrik Øksendal (2008), "Monetary policy under the gold standard – examining the case of Norway, 1893–1914," Norges Bank *Working Paper* 2008/14.

economy had changed, the functioning of the labor market had deteriorated,[15] external trade had become more important, and the share of employment in agriculture had declined. We had become more vulnerable to external economic developments.

The objective of monetary policy continued to be a stable value of money in relation to gold. However, the authorities set a very ambitious goal: they aimed to restore the krone's prewar value, which implied deflation. Moreover, they were more impatient than had been the case after the Napoleonic Wars a hundred years earlier. At that time, the par value of money had been restored over a period of twenty years, but now the authorities achieved the same in a quarter of the time, at considerable real economic cost.[16] We usually refer to this as "parity policy."

The ambition to keep their promise was admirable, but the follow-through lacked flexibility.[17] We might say that

---

[15] See Olav Bjerkholt and Jan F. Qvigstad (2007), "Introduction to Ragnar Frisch's 1933 pamphlet 'Saving and Circulation Regulation,'" in *Revisita di Storia Economica*, Banca d'Italia.

[16] See Øyvind Eitrheim, Jan T. Klovland, and Jan F. Qvigstad (Eds.) (2004), "Historical Monetary Statistics for Norway 1819–2003," Norges Bank's *Occasional Papers* No. 35, p. 293.

[17] However, they were more flexible in September 1931. It only took seven days for Norway to follow the United Kingdom's lead in abandoning the gold standard.

in the 1920s, the central bank adhered rigidly to "the letter of the law."[18]

After World War II, unemployment in the 1920s and 1930s was often associated with the rigidity of "parity policy,"[19] which led to considerable changes in views on economic policy.

The objective of a fixed exchange rate and a gold standard nevertheless remained intact and was achieved. Norway and a number of other countries pegged their currencies to the dollar under the Bretton Woods Agreement. In reality, they also linked the value of their money to gold, since the dollar was linked to gold.[20]

---

[18] There was a fairly general consensus on parity policy in the 1920s. See, for example, Fritz Hodne and Ola Honningdal Grytten (2002), *Norsk økonomi i det 20. århundre* (*The Norwegian economy in the 20th century*), Bergen: Fagbokforlaget, pp. 111–112; and Hermod Skånland (1967), "Det norske kredittmarked siden 1900 (The Norwegian credit market since 1900)," *Samfunnsøkonomiske studier* No. 19, Oslo: Statistics Norway. See also Knut Mykland (Ed.) (1976), *Cappelens Norgeshistorie*, Vol. 13, Oslo: Cappelen p. 86.

[19] For further discussion of parity policy and Norges Bank's role, see Gunhild J. Ecklund (2008), in "Creating a new role for an old Central Bank: The Bank of Norway 1945–1954," Series of Dissertations 2/2008, BI Norwegian School of Management, Oslo, pp. 46–51 and 67–71.

[20] This link to gold was not as strong as when the obligation to redeem in gold applied. Under the Bretton Woods system, countries whose public finances were in disequilibrium, or that allowed inflation to

On Central Banking

The postwar period was marked by the strong conviction that the economy could be fine-tuned by the coordinated use of instruments decided at a centralized level. The value of the krone was pegged to the dollar and to gold while a policy of low interest rates was accompanied by an ample credit supply. This was possible in a highly regulated economy. The positive attitude to regulation probably stemmed from the period of rationing and centralized government during World War II. The system had functioned reasonably well and a regulatory apparatus was already in place.[21]

Internationally, there was a widespread desire to stabilize economic developments, originating in theories published by John Maynard Keynes in the early 1930s. This was part of the background for Norwegian politicians' ambition to fine-tune the economy in Norway. The works of A. W. Phillips,[22] published in 1958, also

rise for other reasons, had to let their exchange rate depreciate against the dollar. When the exchange rate against the dollar fell, the value of money measured in gold decreased.

[21] See Olav Bjerkholt (2008), "Sosialøkonomenes oppmarsj og nasjonalbudsjettet (The rise of the economist and the national budget)," *Samfunnsøkonomen*, Vol. 68, Nos. 6 and 7.

[22] Alban W. Phillips (1958), "The Relation Between Unemployment and the Rate of Change of Money Wage Rates in the United Kingdom, 1861–1957," *Economica*, Vol. 25, No. 100, pp. 283–299.

supported this view. According to Phillips, a country could choose between low unemployment and low inflation. This menu option is often referred to as the Phillips curve. And what kind of "option" was that? Unemployment is real, while inflation is only changes in an index! By formulating the question in this way, the choice was obvious. This analysis had a considerable impact on economic policy in many Western countries.

The global economic situation became difficult into the 1970s, with low growth and high inflation in Norway and other countries. U.S. and European authorities opted to pursue an active countercyclical policy rather than combating inflation. But the trade-off between inflation and unemployment did not hold in the long term, as economists had first thought. Their analyses had not factored in expectation formation. When higher inflation gradually came to be expected by economic agents, it no longer led to lower unemployment.

In his work, Phillips introduced the dilemma of short-term gains and long-term costs in a new area. The benefit was lower unemployment for a period. But confidence that inflation could be kept low would eventually be eroded. The cost was persistently higher inflation. The short-term benefit evaporated along with confidence.

It is easy to see that it can be tempting to exploit the short-term gains even though the long-term costs are known. In 1971, for example, U.S. president Richard Nixon sought higher growth in the money supply and an attendant reduction in unemployment in order to increase his chances of being reelected.[23] He was aware of the inflation problems that would subsequently arise, but his view was that they could be addressed at a later stage. Perhaps he believed that if he were not reelected, the long-term costs would be someone else's problem. The lesson we can learn from this is that a system involving changing governments may be particularly prone to short-term temptations. Finding an effective commitment mechanism is of particular importance in this context.

Because of a lack of fiscal discipline, the Federal Reserve suspended its obligation to redeem dollars for gold in 1971 and the Bretton Woods Agreement collapsed. This was the beginning of a period of inflation and economic instability in many parts of the world, referred to as the decade of the Great Inflation. In Norway, as in other countries, the government moved in practice away from the objective of a permanently

---

[23] Milton Friedman and Rose D. Friedman (1998), *Two Lucky People: Memoirs*, University of Chicago Press, pp. 386–387. More rapid growth in the money supply would imply lower interest rates in the short term.

stable exchange rate.[24] It carried out ten de facto devaluations of the krone in the period 1976–1986,[25] which led to high inflation. Data on price developments in Norway are available back to 1516. Five hundred years of price history show that in historical terms, the inflation period

[24] In 1975, Thomas J. Sargent and Neil Wallace published the article "'Rational' Expectations, the Optimal Monetary Instrument and the Optimal Money Supply Rule," *Journal of Political Economy*, Vol. 83, No. 2, April, pp. 241–254. According to the article, monetary policy had to come as a surprise in order to have any impact on the economy. Expected policy had no effect. This was probably also part of the reason for the acceptance of diverging from promises made, and may explain why transparency was of so little interest to the authorities. Theoretical works published some years later showed that expected and rules-based policy could nonetheless stabilize the economy, provided price and wage rigidity existed. Some examples are: Stanley Fischer (1977), "Long-Term Contracts, Rational Expectations, and the Optimal Money Supply Rule," *Journal of Political Economy*, Vol. 88, No. 1, pp. 191–206; John B. Taylor (1980), "Aggregate Dynamics and Staggered Contracts," *Journal of Political Economy*, Vol. 88, No. 1, pp. 1–24; and Guillermo A. Calvo (1983), "Staggered Prices in a Utility-Maximizing Framework," *Journal of Monetary Economics*, Vol. 12, No. 3, pp. 983–998. Only when these articles were published was the theoretical basis in place for keeping promises while at the same time allowing monetary policy to contribute to stabilizing the economy.

[25] See Qvigstad and Skjæveland, *Stabilitet og langsiktighet. Festskrift til Hermod Skånland* [Stability and longtermism. Festschrift for Hermod Skånland], Oslo: aschehoug.

in the 1970s and 1980s is unique.[26] Previously, periods of high inflation had been associated with government deficits as a result of war and unstable governments. This time, inflation was related to the system of economic policy management.

The era of high inflation must be viewed against the background of the mixed experience of the parity system and reduced weight on keeping promises, ambitious economic stabilization policies, and belief in the validity of the Phillips curve. In addition, the importance of a stable value of money had perhaps lost some of its prominence.

As there are many lawyers present here today, I will venture to comment on a case in your field of expertise: the so-called gold clause case ("Gullklausulsaken").[27] The Norwegian government had issued a number of bonds in the period 1896 to 1909.[28] Many of the bonds

---

[26] See Øyvind Eitrheim in Øyvind Eitrheim and Jan F. Qvigstad (Eds.) (2005), "Tilbakeblikk på norsk pengehistorie. Konferanse 7. juni 2005 på Bogstad gård (Norwegian monetary history in retrospect. Conference, 7 June 2005, Oslo)," Norges Bank's *Occasional Papers* No. 37.

[27] Henrik Bahr (1962), "Høyesteretts dom i gullklausulsaken (The Supreme Court ruling in the gold clause case)," *Lov og Rett*, Vol. 1, No. 5, pp. 193–211.

[28] Two government-guaranteed banks had also issued bonds.

were held by French moneylenders. The bonds were issued in the gold standard period and the moneylenders were promised repayment in "monnaie d'or." When the bonds matured, the Norwegian government wanted to make the repayment in banknotes that had lost much of their value. This implied a devaluation that could perhaps be compared to the devaluation under Henry VIII. The French moneylenders refused the offer and the case finally came before the Supreme Court in 1962. In their voting, the Supreme Court gave weight to a law from 1923, which stated that the gold clause, that is, repayment in gold money, did not apply if the obligation to redeem banknotes for gold had been suspended, which it had been permanently in 1931. In the explanation of its ruling, the Supreme Court also referred to "vital national interests." It would cost Norwegian taxpayers far too much to repay the gold money that had been borrowed sixty years earlier.

It would be far too pretentious of me to offer an opinion on the court ruling as such. What makes this case interesting in the light of today's topic is that in the Supreme Court's assessment of "vital national interests," there is no discussion of what the nation's interests are in the short term versus the long term. However, it must be added that it is probably not easy for a court to review other government authorities' assessments of this point.

There is also the question of whether this falls within the Court's purview.

Modern Monetary Policy: A Promise Both Possible and Right to Keep

The theoretical breakthrough by Kydland and Prescott and the era of high inflation eventually had implications for practical policy. It was observed that countries where weight was given to low inflation, such as Germany, had recorded favorable economic developments.

Since the beginning of the 1980s, there has been a broad international consensus that monetary policy must be geared toward price stability. This paradigm shift also reached Norway, but not until the end of the 1980s. The government recognized that the frequently repeated devaluations had become ineffectual. Confidence had been lost. In Norway, inflation had also soared without a fall in unemployment. Even if it was costly to restore credibility, in reality we had no choice.[29] The alternative was to bring the country even closer to

---

[29] The new recognition that policy should be based on confidence rather than a series of surprises reflects the influence of theoretical developments on practical policy, cf. footnote 24.

the brink of financial chaos and runaway inflation. The devaluation in 1986 would be the last in the series.

Internationally, the 1980s ushered in three innovations that would become decisive for the shaping of modern monetary policy as we know it.

First, market deregulation led to freer cross-border capital flows. Promises could no longer be relegated to the future. Failing credibility was promptly reflected in higher interest rates and weaker exchange rates. Nixon's disinflation plan to bring down inflation at some point in the future would have had immediate consequences. On the other hand, it also became clear that a credible and transparent monetary policy could be more effective precisely thanks to financial markets' swift reactions.[30]

Second, the notion of central bank autonomy regained favor. Political authorities who wanted to show the world that they were committed to delivering their promise of price stability did as Ulysses and let themselves be bound to the mast. The mechanism was central bank independence and Norway was no exception. The new Norges Bank Act of 1985 gave Norges Bank the authority to set the

---

[30] In recent times, central banks throughout the world have become more independent but at the same time more transparent and predictable in their communication with other economic agents. This is also related to the new recognition referred to in footnote 24.

interest rate. Democratic control is now ensured through a clear mandate defined by the government for the central bank's conduct of monetary policy. The political authorities can verify the central bank's compliance with the mandate without deciding on the use of the instrument.[31]

The third innovation sprang out of New Zealand. In connection with economic reforms, the authorities had introduced fiscal performance targets. They then started searching for good and realistic performance targets for monetary policy. They found that what monetary policy should deliver was stable inflation in the medium term – New Zealand introduced a so-called inflation target for monetary policy.[32]

What is the difference between what is referred to as inflation targeting and the former policy of parity?

---

[31] Norges Bank reports on the conduct of monetary policy in its *Monetary Policy Report* and *Annual Report*. Norges Bank's reporting obligations are set out in Article 75c of the Constitution and Section 3 of the Norges Bank Act. The *Annual Report* is submitted to the Ministry of Finance, presented to the King in Council and communicated to the Storting in the Government Credit Report. The Governor of Norges Bank also appears at open hearings of the Standing Committee on Finance and Economic Affairs.

[32] The objective of EMU is consumer price stability in member countries as a whole, rather than stable prices in individual countries. The arguments for a stable value of money are the same as for Norway.

On Keeping Promises

Let me explain the difference using a stylized example. Assume that the price index has been 100 over a longer period. The price level is thus stable. An increase in, say, energy prices then occurs and the index moves up to 105. Energy has become more expensive in relation to other goods. Under the parity system, other prices had to be reduced to move the index back to 100. This could require a substantial decline in output and employment, as was the case in the interwar years. Under an inflation targeting regime, it would in this example be accepted that the index remained at 105. The central bank would ensure that economic agents did not believe that inflation of 5 percent – an index with an annual rise of 5 percent – had become the normal level, thereby preventing such a belief from affecting their behavior. Under an inflation targeting regime, the central bank would accept, when shocks occur, a price increase without other prices having to be reduced. A promise made under an inflation-targeting regime is easier to keep when the economy is exposed to major shocks than a promise made under a parity system.[33]

---

[33] Another difference is that under parity policy the authorities stabilized the price of gold and not the price of a basket of representative goods – the consumer price index. Today, stabilization of the consumer price index would be described as price level targeting.

On Central Banking

From 1986 until the beginning of the 1990s, Norway maintained a fixed exchange rate against European currencies without devaluations. In practice, this meant that Norway also had to pursue the same inflation goal as those countries. In autumn 1992, the fixed exchange rate regime collapsed. Even if we no longer operated a formal fixed exchange rate system, in the following years monetary policy was still oriented toward maintaining a stable exchange rate at all times.[34] However, the currency turbulence in the latter part of summer 1998 demonstrated that, like other central banks, Norges Bank could not make good on the promise to maintain a stable exchange

Inflation targeting, on the other hand, implies stabilization of the *changes* in the consumer price index. There is also a difference in that there is no longer any redemption obligation. Confidence is not based on gold reserves, but more generally on responsible economic policy as a basis for achieving the inflation target through the active use of the interest rate.

[34] At that time, little academic research was available on alternatives to a fixed exchange rate regime or money supply targeting. Leading politicians and economists were sceptical about the idea of abandoning the fixed exchange rate regime. Money supply targeting was regarded as out of the question because of instability in the money supply. John Taylor's works on interest rate rules that could contribute to stabilizing inflation and the real economy, through transparency and predictability, were not published until 1993 (John B. Taylor, "Discretion versus Policy Rules in Practice," *Carnegie-Rochester Series on Public Policy*, Vol. 39, pp. 195–214).

rate from hour to hour, day to day, or week to week. Domestic economic considerations indicated that there were limits to how high the interest rate could be set in support of the krone exchange rate. An excessively high interest rate would not have been credible since it would have resulted in an excessively sharp downswing in domestic economic activity.

In August 1998, Norges Bank shifted policy to setting the interest rate with a view to keeping inflation low and stable over time.[35] The shift in monetary policy was explained in articles and statements in early winter 1999.[36] The inflation target was finally formalized in a

[35] Kjell Storvik (1998), "Aktuelle økonomiske og pengepolitiske problemstillinger (Current economic and monetary policy issues)," Lecture at Forex Norway's 43rd general assembly, 28 August 1998. See www.norges-bank.no. Norges Bank was prepared for a change in regime; cf. the discussions in Anne Berit Christiansen and Jan F. Qvigstad (Eds.) (1997), *Choosing a Monetary Policy Target*, Oslo: Universitetsforlaget; and Jan F. Qvigstad and Øistein Røisland (Eds.) (2000), *Perspektiver på pengepolitikken (Monetary policy perspectives)*, Oslo: Gyldendal Akademisk. A workshop entitled "The Conduct of Monetary Policy in Open Economies" was also held at the Norwegian Academy of Science and Letters in October 2000.

[36] Article in the daily newspaper *Aftenposten* on 5 January 1999 in connection with the appointment of Svein Gjedrem as governor of Norges Bank; lecture by Svein Gjedrem, Gausdal, 28 January 1999: "Utfordringer i den økonomiske politikken (Challenges to

new regulation on monetary policy in 2001, a good eleven years after New Zealand, nine years after the United Kingdom, and eight years after Sweden.

The mandate for Norges Bank states that monetary policy shall, in addition to securing price stability, contribute to stabilizing output and employment. It is possible to give weight to cyclical fluctuations in interest rate setting, and to new information, as long as there is confidence that inflation remains near the target. The central bank's announced interest rate strategy ahead will be adjusted as new information emerges. This stands in contrast to the parity system, which was more rigid.

The authorities cannot systematically allow policy to be more expansionary than announced to bring down unemployment. As Kydland and Prescott demonstrated, this would in the long term lead to higher inflation without lower unemployment. Credibility hinges on the active use of the interest rate to attain the target.

The lawyer and economist Michael Woodford has pointed out that in order to keep your word it is not enough to make a promise today and keep this promise

economic policy)"; and article by Svein Gjedrem in *Aftenposten* 4 May 1999: "Utfordringer i pengepolitikken (Challenges to economic policy)."

tomorrow.[37] When making interest rate forecasts, we must also take into consideration the promises made yesterday. Only then can we fully use expectations to stabilize the economy optimally. This is referred to as monetary policy from a timeless perspective.[38] My understanding is that a person will likewise look both backward and forward when interpreting the laws of a society. It is Norwegian court practice for judges to consider precedent effects and case law when interpreting legislation.

Today there is general consensus that price stability is not only the best contribution that monetary policy can make to economic stability over time, but perhaps also the only promise the central bank can actually deliver.

Today's Financial Crisis

At present, the world is in the throes of a severe financial crisis – the deepest crisis since the 1930s. Many foreign

[37] Michael Woodford (2003), *Interest and Prices*, Princeton University Press.

[38] Michael Woodford (2003) points out that the central bank's announced interest rate strategy can be adjusted as new information becomes available. However, in order to maintain confidence in the announced interest rate path and for it to be useful, the public must not have reason to expect *systematic* deviations.

banks have suffered large losses and a sense of fear is prevailing. We are entering a global economic recession. The authorities are taking action to restore confidence in the financial industry. Macroeconomic policy measures are aimed at limiting the crisis-related effects on the real economy. It is clear that regulatory improvements will eventually be needed so that the financial industry can assume a greater role in safeguarding its own credibility.

The credibility of central banks is also being tested in this situation. In dramatic cases, such as Iceland, we are again seeing an example of runaway inflation when confidence in government finances is severely impaired. In this situation, inflation targeting at the central bank of Iceland did not suffice. In Iceland, the problems stemmed from an oversized financial industry and fundamental macroeconomic imbalances. When the banks encountered problems, the authorities provided support in an attempt to secure a functioning financial system. As the Icelandic state did not have the financial strength to take over the banks' total commitments, confidence in its currency and monetary policy was also shattered without the central bank being able to redress the situation.

The financial crisis is a global one, and the Norwegian economy will be affected. However, our country is in a sound position to curb crisis-related effects. In Norway, government finances are healthy, the banking system is solid, and there is confidence that monetary policy will continue to maintain a stable value of money. This means that we can use the interest rate actively. We have already reduced it in two increments, by a total of 1 percentage point, and we are willing to use the interest rate to a further extent if necessary.

Central banks still face many unknowns about economic behavior. There is nothing in our history that indicates that monetary policy, or any economic policy for that matter, has found its final form. But there is one certainty: keeping promises and creating confidence are fundamental both for monetary policy and more generally for growth and development.

CHAPTER TWO

On Transparency

Introduction

Norges Bank's Executive Board has decided that the key policy rate now should be 1.5 percent.[*] If economic developments are broadly in line with projections, the appropriate key policy rate will be 2.75 percent around the end of next year.

* Ida Wolden Bache, Amund Holmsen, Marie Norum Lerbak, and Øistein Røisland provided valuable assistance in preparing this lecture. I would also like to thank Helle Snellingen for her contribution to the translation of the Norwegian text into English.

On Transparency

If I had made this statement ten years ago, it would have constituted a breach of confidentiality.[1] Norges Bank considered this to be highly sensitive information. Had I been deputy chairman of the U.S. Federal Reserve Board twenty years ago, I would not even have been entitled to reveal the latest interest rate decision.[2] Today, this sounds

---

[1] The duty of confidentiality for Norges Bank employees is laid down in Section 12 of the Norges Bank Act. Violation of the duty of confidentiality is punishable under the General Civil Penal Code: "Any person who wilfully or through gross negligence violates a duty of secrecy which in accordance with any statutory provision or valid directive is a consequence of his service or work for any state or municipal body shall be liable to fines or imprisonment for a term not exceeding six months" (Section 121, first paragraph of the General Civil Penal Code).

[2] In 1975, David R. Merrill, a law student, instigated legal proceedings against the Federal Open Market Committee (FOMC) in the United States, charging that the FOMC violated the Freedom of Information Act by deferring public disclosure of its interest rate decision by ninety days. The case was eventually heard by the Supreme Court. The Supreme Court ruled that the Federal Reserve could continue its practice if it could provide an adequate explanation showing that immediate disclosure would significantly harm the government's monetary functions or commercial interests. The Supreme Court left the assessment of this explanation to the district court. The district court concluded that it lacked the expertise necessary to substitute its judgment for that of the FOMC and the Federal Reserve did not begin to release its monetary policy decisions on the same day until 1994. See Marvin Goodfriend (1986), "Monetary

rather odd. Transparency is now taken for granted among central banks and in other areas of society.

In London in 1780, the Bank of England was put to a test. In Parliament, Lord Gorden attempted to stop a bill to restore civil rights to Catholics.[3] He drew support from large numbers. Rioting led to the destruction of several public buildings. When an attack was launched against the Bank of England, the building was secured like a fortress and withstood the onslaught, hence the phrase "as safe as the Bank of England." Through the years, the phrase has been simplified into "as safe as the bank." As banks and central banks store gold and money in their vaults, their edifices have always been solid, protected by thick walls. In a figurative sense, it might be said that a safe and credible national monetary value relied for a long time on thick central bank walls insulating its internal workings from the general public.

Until our time, central banks have been closed, both physically and figuratively. Central banks were shrouded in an aura of mystique, which they probably had a hand in perpetuating. Central bank governors worldwide

mystique: secrecy and central banking," *Journal of Monetary Economics*, Vol. 17, No. 1, pp. 63–92.

[3] The bill also enabled Catholics to serve in the British army. British military forces were involved in conflicts in many countries at the time and needed more manpower. See A. Andréadès (1966), *History of the Bank of England 1640–1903*, 4th edition, Frank Cass & co.

refrained from saying too much, and what they did say often sounded cryptic.

In Norway, monetary policy was probably also perceived by many as something mysterious and remote. In the Festschrift for former Norges Bank governor Hermod Skånland, Professor Preben Munthe writes the following:

> There is a tradition that expects central bank governors to be parsimonious with words. This built up the aura that should surround a man in that position. He possessed knowledge about the secret black box – monetary policy with a capital M – and how it functioned. Without asking others, he changed the discount rate and thereby intervened in the economy with authority and deep insight. On seldom occasions did he step down from his cloud of wisdom to impart life's economic truths to a gaping public.[4]

A change in views and practices relating to transparency first occurred in recent years, both in Norway and in other countries.[5] It can safely be said that the change has been swift and radical. Today, most central banks are open about (i) the *objective* of monetary policy, (ii) its

---

[4] Preben Munthe (1994), "Økonomen (The Economist)," in Jan. F Qvigstad, Sigbjørn Atle Berg, and Kjell Storvik (eds.), *Stabilitet og langsiktighet: festskrift til Hermod Skånland (Stability and a long-term perspective: Festschrift for Hermod Skånland)*, Aschehoug, p. 73.

[5] See, for example, Alan S. Blinder, Michael Ehrmann, Marcel Fratzscher, Jakob De Haan, and David-Jan Jansen (2008), "Central Bank Communication and Monetary Policy: A Survey of Theory and Evidence," *Journal of Economic Literature*, Vol. 46, No. 4, pp. 910–945; and Petra M. Geraats (2002), "Central Bank Transparency," *The Economic Journal*, Vol. 112 (November), pp. F532–F556.

strategy for reaching the objective, and (iii) the *background* for and the *process* behind interest rate decisions.

Norges Bank is no exception in this respect. In some areas, Norges Bank has gone further than others. For example, Norges Bank is one of the few central banks in the world that publishes forecasts of its own interest rate decisions.[6]

What then can explain this tendency toward greater transparency? I would highlight two main reasons. First, there has been a general trend in society toward greater transparency. Second, economic thinking has changed considerably. Simplifying somewhat, the former view was that monetary policy operated effectively by *surprising* economic agents. Today, economic theory posits that monetary policy works best if it is *predictable*.

I will come back to the economic theory, but allow me to start by describing some changes in society at large.

Transparency of Economic Policy

The economic crisis in the 1930s shattered confidence in free market forces. Markets had to be controlled. The British economist John Maynard Keynes was working

---

[6] See, for example, Ralph Atkins (2007), "Central bankers eye Norway's clarity on rates," *Financial Times*, 2 March, p. 11, and Michael Woodford (2007), "The Case for Forecast Targeting as a Monetary Policy Strategy," *Journal of Economic Perspectives*, Vol. 21, No. 4, pp. 3–24.

on ways of regulating and improving markets. Prominent Norwegian economists, with Ragnar Frisch at the fore, went even further. They advocated that the market economy must be replaced by a planned economy. Ambitions were high. One could almost say that transparency, in carefully selected portions, was a tactical tool.[7] It reached a head in 1973 when a commission led by Hermod Skånland proposed the establishment of an incomes-policy council that was to decide the limits for wage growth in Norway.[8]

But the proposal was not in tune with the new views that were already taking root in society. The council was never established. Domestic and international developments in the 1970s weakened the conviction that the economy could be fine-tuned. While market failure was the main concern earlier, focus now shifted to *regulatory failure*. The political pendulum swung away from government control

---

[7] In 1959, Petter Jacob Bjerve, then director general of Statistics Norway, wrote that "Apparently, the question of whether national budgets should be published involved an optimum problem: considering both advantages and disadvantages of publishing, any cabinet will probably decide what to publish so as to achieve best possible results of its policy, according to the social preferences of the cabinet." See Petter Jacob Bjerve (1959), *Planning in Norway 1947–1956*, North-Holland Publishing Company, p. 352.

[8] See NOU (Official Norwegian Report) 1973:36 *Om prisproblemene (On price problems)*.

and toward market liberalization.[9] When decision making was to be decentralized, it was important that the decision makers acted in line with the overriding policy objectives. New transparency and disclosure requirements were designed to this end. The requirements were largely set out in the Public Administration Act of 1967 and the Freedom of Information Act of 1970.

Today, transparency and disclosure requirements also apply to Norwegian enterprises, particularly to listed companies.[10] The legislation is to ensure that all shareholders receive adequate, correct, and timely information from the company. Companies must be open and assure equal treatment of all owners. Well-functioning equity markets rely on confidence that everyone has access to the same information about the company.

Transparency Is Natural in a Democracy

Transparency is natural in a democracy and is important to ensure accountability among decision makers. The

---

[9] For an account of economic policy in Norway in the twentieth century, see Tore Jørgen Hanisch, Espen Søilen, and Gunhild J. Ecklund (1999), *Norsk økonomisk politikk i det 20. århundre. Verdivalg i en åpen økonomi (Economic policy in Norway in the 20th century. Ethics in an open economy)*, Høyskoleforlaget.

[10] See, i.e., chapter 5 in the Norwegian Act on Securities Trading.

On Transparency

Danish Nobel laureate in physics Niels Bohr supposedly once stated that "The best weapon of a dictatorship is secrecy, but the best weapon of a democracy should be the weapon of *openness*."

Yesterday was the twentieth anniversary of the fall of the Berlin Wall. This event has become a symbol of the fall of the iron curtain. We recall from those times the Russian word *glasnost*, which means openness. Mikhail Gorbachev sought to modernize the Soviet Union and used glasnost as a means of reducing corruption and abuse of power. In western democracies, the term "glasnost" took on a broader meaning, and was associated with detente between East and West in the 1980s.[11]

As mentioned, the shift toward a more decentralized economy both in Norway and abroad reflected the failure of centralized planning. Monetary policy is an important component of the economic policy framework.[12] In my

[11] In Norway, the concept is also associated with Jahn Teigen's contribution "Glasnost" in the national final of the Eurovision Song Contest 1988.

[12] As a response to the financial crises that started in the fall of 2008, the government wrote in a report to the Storting 26 January 2009: "Monetary policy is the first line of defence in countering a setback in the economy." See Report No. 37 (2008–2009) to the Storting (Norwegian parliament) "Om endringer i statsbudsjettet 2009 med

lecture "On Keeping Promises,"[13] I noted that it can be demanding for the political authorities to ensure price stability because *low* interest rates are often more popular than *high* interest rates. An *appropriate* interest rate may therefore be demanding to set in government corridors.[14] Most government authorities in democratic countries have solved this problem by delegating interest rate setting to an independent central bank.

But how can the conduct of monetary policy, which has such far-reaching consequences for so many, be delegated in a democratic country? How is one to ensure that decisions are in line with the interests of society? These questions become more relevant when there is more room for judgment in interest rate setting.

When the operational objective was a fixed exchange rate, the room for judgment was very limited. Norges

tiltak for arbeid (On changes in the 2009 Budget and labour measures)," Ministry of Finance, p. 6.

[13] The lecture entitled "On Keeping Promises," remarks by Endre Stavang and Henrik Syse, and Francis Sejersted's summary of the debate have been published in Norges Bank Occasional Papers, No. 39, 2009.

[14] This is discussed by Finn Kydland, who won the 2004 Nobel Prize in Economics with Edward Prescott for their analysis of the problems of economic planning. See Finn Kydland and Edward Prescott (1977), "Rules Rather Than Discretion: The Inconsistency of Optimal Plans," *Journal of Political Economy*, Vol. 85, No. 3, pp. 473–491.

On Transparency

Bank's task was to maintain a fixed krone exchange rate. Monetary policy was more or less on "autopilot." In a narrow sense, this was a very open policy. The public could at all times observe the krone exchange rate and monitor that the Bank was performing its duty. Many of you perhaps remember the era when a dollar cost 7 kroner and 14 øre.[15] On the basis of purely democratic considerations, there was little need for transparency about the *assessments* underlying the use of instruments.

The exchange rate was fixed, but occasionally the target value was adjusted. At those times the cards were held close to the breast. On occasion it was even necessary to break the eighth commandment (that is, to lie). Around the end of 1986, journalists in the newspaper Nordlys were asked to take a retrospective look at the past year. One of them recalled an interview with the state secretary of the Ministry of Finance, Bjørn Skogstad

[15] The central value of the Norwegian Krone against the U.S. dollar was 7.14 from 18 September 1949 to 15 August 1971. See addendum, prepared by Ragna Alstadheim, to Jan F. Qvigstad, and Arent Skjæveland (1994), "Valutakursregimer – historiske erfaringer og fremtidige utfordringer (Exchange rate regimes – historical experiences and future challenges)" in Jan. F Qvigstad, Sigbjørn Atle Berg and Kjell Storvik (eds.), *Stabilitet og langsiktighet. Festskrift til Hermod Skånland (Stability and a long-term perspective. Festschrift for Hermod Skånland)*, Aschehoug.

Aamo. In the interview Skogstad Aamo flatly denied rumors of a krone devaluation. But before the interview was printed, the news agency NTB reported that the krone had been devalued by 12 percent.[16] Perhaps the journalist was disappointed but Skogstad Aamo was not criticized for breaking the eighth commandment.

Over the last decade, the objective of monetary policy has not been a fixed krone exchange rate, but price stability through low and stable inflation.[17] According to the monetary policy regulation, the objective is inflation of close to 2.5 percent over time. But how long is "over time"? And what is "close to 2.5 percent"? With these formulations, it is no longer that easy to evaluate monetary policy. There are several reasons for this. First, it takes up to one to two years for a change in the interest rate to feed through to inflation. Second, inflation is not only influenced by the interest rate. For example, precipitation levels can have a strong impact on electricity prices. Third, we set interest rates also with the aim of promoting stability in output and employment. If the economy is

[16] This story is reported in the article "Borten i fokus og bestillingsverk (Borten in focus and commissioned works)," *Aftenposten*, 3 January 1987.

[17] See, for example, Report No. 29 (2000–2001) to the Storting from the Ministry of Finance and the Regulation on Monetary Policy from 29 March 2001.

exposed to severe shocks, we may at times seek to bring inflation rapidly back to target, while under other conditions we deliberately choose a longer horizon.

An evaluation of monetary policy cannot therefore be based on the latest figures for inflation. Instead, one must check whether average inflation over a somewhat longer period has been close to 2.5 percent. Measuring performance is possible, but can only be done with a time lag.[18]

The combination of (i) delegated authority to conduct policy, (ii) room for discretion, and (iii) difficulties in the day-to-day monitoring of results implies a risk of a democratic deficit. Transparency and disclosure are the institutional solution to this problem. Even if a central bank is independent in the conduct of monetary policy, it must be accountable to government. We must be measured on our performance, but also on our assessments and decisions. This requires transparency. The need for transparency therefore depends on the monetary policy regime. Internationally, there is also a tendency for inflation-targeting central banks to be

---

[18] Lars E. O. Svensson, Deputy Governor at Sveriges Riksbank, has argued that it is possible to evaluate monetary policy actions ex ante. See Lars E. O. Svensson (2009), "Policy Expectations and Policy Evaluations: The Role of Transparency and Communication," address at the conference "Tio år med självständig Riksbank (Ten years with an independent Riksbank)," 11 September 2009.

more transparent than those in countries with a fixed exchange rate regime.[19]

Transparency about Norges Bank's activity is required by law. When the Storting (Norwegian parliament) amended §100 on the freedom of expression in the Constitution, the freedom of information principle was enshrined in the Constitution.[20] This was the first time this article had been amended since 1814. The legislative amendments were partly based on the proposals of the Freedom of Expression Commission, which was headed by Professor Francis Sejersted.[21] In addition, Norges Bank is subject to a transparency requirement in the Freedom of Information Act and the Act on Norges Bank and the Monetary System.[22]

---

[19] See Nergiz Dincer and Barry Eichengreen (2009), "Central Bank Transparency: Causes, Consequences and Updates," NBER Working Paper 14791 and Petra M. Geraats (2009), "Trends in Monetary Policy Transparency," *International Finance*, Vol. 12, No. 2, pp. 235–268.

[20] The new legal text establishes the so-called principle of free access to public records, which provides public access to central and local government documents and the right to be present at sittings of the courts and of administrative bodies elected by the people.

[21] NOU (Official Norwegian Report) 1999:27 "Ytringsfrihed bør finde Sted (There shall be freedom of expression)." Sejersted was awarded the Ossietzky Prize for his contribution to freedom of expression in 2008.

[22] In the Norges Bank Act of 1985, Norges Bank is required to "inform the public of the assessments on which monetary policy decisions are

On Transparency

In some areas, we are even more transparent than what is required by law. Norges Bank's *Monetary Policy Report* includes a thorough account of our assessments of economic developments and interest rate setting. As mentioned in the Introduction, we even publish a forecast for our future interest rate decisions. After each monetary policy meeting, a press conference is held where we explain the interest rate decision and answer questions from journalists. The press conference is webcast live and usually broadcast on TV. People can subscribe to receive an SMS message about interest rate decisions, and Norges Bank was apparently the first central bank to publish its interest rate decisions on Twitter.

International developments have made it prestigious for central banks to be as open as possible. But transparency cannot be a goal in itself. Our responsibility is to conduct an effective monetary policy in line with the objectives laid down by the political authorities. Transparency beyond that necessary to ensure

based." In October 2009, a new government communications policy was laid down by the Ministry of Government Administration and Reform, promoting transparency as an important principle of good communication. The government's communication is required to be open, clear, and accessible. The government is also required to ensure that relevant information reaches the relevant parties and that the information is adapted to the relevant target groups.

democratic accountability is a goal derived from the main goal of conducting an optimal monetary policy.

Modern Economic Theory Argues in Favor of Transparency

I mentioned that the previous view was that monetary policy operated by surprising economic agents, while the prevailing view is that it works best by being predictable. According to modern economic theory, economic decisions are heavily influenced by *expectations*.[23] This has also become an important recognition in economic policy. Today's key rate is important, but even more important is the expected key interest rate ahead. When the owner of a firm takes up a loan to build a new factory, the expected interest rate over the life of the loan is taken into account. When the key rate was reduced sharply in autumn last year, we sought to communicate that the interest rate would remain low for a period and not be raised back to the former level already the following week or month.

According to theory monetary policy to a large extent seeks to affect expectations. We believe that by being

---

[23] See, for example, Michael Woodford (2005), "Central-Bank Communication and Policy Effectiveness," in *The Greenspan Era: Lessons for the Future*, Federal Reserve Bank of Kansas City, pp. 399–474

transparent about our own interest rate forecasts, it is easier to influence expectations. This enhances the effectiveness of monetary policy.

But the interest rate forecast is a forecast, and not a promise. The future is uncertain. Actual interest rate developments may therefore deviate from our forecasts. We try to be open about how we will react if new information implies a different interest rate path.

Transparency about Norges Bank's reaction pattern is a necessary element in the interaction with fiscal policy. It is important that the government and the Storting know the central bank's response pattern when the size of government budgets is decided. It is also an advantage for the social partners take this into account.

Our view on transparency and good communication is inspired by Wim Duisenberg, the first President of the European Central Bank. His definition of transparency was that "the external communication should reflect the internal deliberations."[24]

We have all experienced that memory is imperfect. The easiest approach is therefore to employ the

---

[24] Willem F. Duisenberg (2001), "The ECB's monetary policy strategy and the quantitative definition of price stability," Letter of Dr. W. F. Duisenberg, President of the ECB to the Chairperson of the Committee on Economic and Monetary Affairs, 13 December 2001.

same narrative everywhere. What we say in the Executive Board is also what we say to the Minister of Finance, at press conferences, and in speeches. Earlier we asked ourselves: Are there any particular reasons to release this information? Now we ask ourselves whether there are any particular reasons *not* to be open. The Duisenberg principle is a practical guideline for us.

Some studies show that transparency about the monetary policy target helps anchor inflation expectations.[25] The more credible monetary policy is, the more effective the interest rate will be in stabilizing output and employment.[26]

Transparency provides good incentives. When we publish our analyses, we tend to make an even greater effort to

---

[25] See for example Georgios Chortareas, David Stasavage, and Gabriel Sterne (2002), "Monetary Policy Transparency, Inflation and the Sacrifice Ratio," *International Journal of Finance & Economics*, Vol. 7, pp. 141–155, and Nergiz Dincer and Barry Eichengreen (2009), "Central Bank Transparency: Causes, Consequences and Updates," NBER Working Paper 14791.

[26] Openness about how the interest rate is set also seems to generate less volatility in financial markets at the time of monetary policy meetings, resulting in more stable market rates. See, for example, Richild Moessner and William R. Nelson (2008), "Central bank policy rate guidance and financial market functioning," *International Journal of Central Banking*, Vol. 4, No. 4, pp. 193–226, and Amund Holmsen, Jan F. Qvigstad, Øistein Røisland, and Kristin Solberg-Johansen (2008), "Communicating Monetary Policy Intentions: The Case of Norges Bank," Norges Bank Working Paper, 2008/20.

ensure the quality of the analysis. Open external communication also places demands on our communication skills. I am certain that many teachers and lecturers would agree that teaching not only is a means of conveying knowledge to students, but also provides the lecturer with a deeper understanding of the subject. The same applies to central bankers. External communication of our analyses has certainly not reduced our competence as economists.

How Transparent Should the Central Bank Be?

How open should we be? Maximum transparency about Norges Bank's decisions would imply filming the Executive Board's meetings and webcasting them live. In addition, we could perhaps have installed cameras and microphones in some of the offices and meeting rooms in Norges Bank where the analyses are conducted that form the background for the Executive Board's decisions. Perhaps I am old-fashioned, but I think that a reality series about Norges Bank would not be particularly entertaining and would not foster particularly good decision making.

Maximum transparency is probably not optimal, but how far should we go? There is no absolute answer to this. In the following, I will discuss several considerations that must be taken into account.

Should we publish voting records and the minutes of the Executive Board's deliberations? Central banks have chosen different solutions. In Sweden, the central bank publishes the voting records and provides an extensive report with the views of members by name. The Bank of England publishes a similar report of the minutes, but members remain anonymous. Norges Bank does not publish a report of the minutes of the Executive Board's deliberations, but instead publishes a detailed account explaining the Executive Board's background for the interest rate decision. The interest rate decision is based on a strategy that is described in the *Monetary Policy Report*. The Report also presents the analyses underlying the strategy. The basis for interest rate decisions is thus available to the general public.

The difference in practices partly reflects the different character of the monetary policy committees in the three countries.[27] Sveriges Riksbank and the Bank of England have committees that are referred to as "individualistic committees." Each member is individually responsible for his/her vote, and the decision is normally decided by majority voting. In Norway, the Executive Board is more of a "collegial committee," where the members are unanimous in their

[27] See Alan S. Blinder (2007), "Monetary Policy by Committee: Why and How?," *European Journal of Political Economy*, Vol. 23, No. 1, pp. 106–127, and Alan S. Blinder (2008), "On the Design of Monetary Policy Committees," Norges Bank Working Paper, 2008/6.

decision.[28] The system of the European Central Bank (ECB) is of the same type. One cannot have both a collegial committee and minutes with individual views.

    If all members publicly explain their own views, communication may become unclear. Alan Blinder, former vice chairman of the Federal Reserve and now professor at Princeton University, argues that "a central bank that speaks with a cacophony of voices may, in effect, have no voice at all."[29]

There is also another argument in favor of unanimous decisions. Central banks are important social institutions, which should not be too closely linked to individuals but should have a public identity. The institution and its mandate should take precedence over the individuals who occupy positions for limited periods.[30]

---

[28] The Executive Board at Norges Bank consists of seven members, appointed by the King in Council. The Governor and Deputy Governor serve as chairman and deputy chairman, respectively, of the Executive Board. They are appointed to full-time positions for a term of six years. The other five members are appointed for four-year terms and are not employees of Norges Bank.

[29] Alan S. Blinder (2007), "Monetary Policy by Committee: Why and How?," *European Journal of Political Economy*, Vol. 23, No. 1, p. 114.

[30] See, for example, Otmar Issing (2005), "Communication, Transparency, Accountability: Monetary Policy in the Twenty-First Century," *Federal Reserve Bank of St. Louis Review*, Vol. 87, No. 2, p. 73.

There is no formula for deciding which system is best. Each system has its strengths and weaknesses. Detailed meeting minutes ensure accountability among committee members. This may give rise to good incentives. On the other hand, such transparency may inhibit the actual discussion. Members may come to meetings with predrafted statements, impairing a constructive exchange of views.

Researchers have compared tapes of the Fed's Federal Open Market Committee (FOMC) meetings before and after it was decided that the minutes should be published.[31] The tapes show that the form of discussion changed. During the period following the decision to publish the minutes, there was a greater tendency for members to read prepared statements.

Detailed minutes also entail a risk of moving the real discussion from the official meeting into closed rooms. In that case, a real increase in transparency has not been achieved. The United States was aware of this risk and introduced legislation to prevent such informal meetings. They called this law the "Government in the Sunshine Act,"[32] where the name symbolizes that important

---

[31] Ellen E. Meade and David Stasavage (2008), "Publicity of Debate and the Incentive to Dissent: Evidence from the US Federal Reserve," *The Economic Journal*, Vol. 118, pp. 695–717.

[32] Government in the Sunshine Act (5 U.S.C. 552b).

decisions should be made in the public light. The law defines a meeting as a consultation between a quorum of committee members. Stretching it somewhat, this means that if some members are chatting in the corridor, they must stop talking about the interest rate and start talking about the weather if the group grows to a certain size.

The notion that increased transparency can hamper a free exchange of views is not new. The delegates to the Constitutional Convention in Philadelphia in 1787 decided to veil the deliberations in secrecy. According to the Virginia delegate James Madison, who later became the fourth U.S. president, secrecy was crucial for succeeding in the work on the U.S. Constitution. He argued that full disclosure would fuel reluctance among delegates to express their true opinions. Jon Elster has explored various aspects of transparency and constitutions in his research. He notes that even if secrecy can lead to a freer discussion, it can also lead to negotiations based on vested interests.[33] Threats and power struggles can be effective behind closed doors, but rarely tolerate public scrutiny.

The arguments that were used in Philadelphia can be found in the debate on public disclosure of

---

[33] See Jon Elster (1995), "Forces and Mechanisms in the Constitution-Making Process," *Duke Law Journal*, Vol. 45, No. 2, pp. 364–396.

government papers and cabinet deliberations. In a supreme court ruling from 1994, the first-voting judge Steinar Tjomsland wrote: "The possibility that governments should testify before the court . . . could inhibit free political exchange of information and debate."[34]

If we today even know what Tjomsland wrote, it is because the Supreme Court's doors were opened in 1863. The law on transparent voting in the Supreme Court was adopted after a nearly fifty-year conflict between the Storting and the other two branches of government.[35] In 1821, Christian Magnus Falsen put forward a proposal for the public disclosure of voting records in the Supreme Court.[36] He argued that public disclosure was "the most effective means of ensuring confidence and respect for any government authority is by awakening a noble pride among senior civil servants and hence instilling in them respect for the voice of the people."[37] The Supreme Court

---

[34] Norsk Retstidende (Norwegian journal of law) 1994–1036, p. 1044.

[35] The Storting had adopted a bill on transparency in the voting process four times since 1818, but assent to the bill was refused each time.

[36] Guthorm Immanuel Hallager (1935), *Norges høiesteret: 1815–1915* (*The Supreme Court of Norway: 1815–1915*), H. Aschehoug & Co, p. 131.

[37] See parliamentary deliberations for August 1821, Part 5, Addendum, p. 119.

had a different view and argued that it could undermine confidence in the Court if the public discovered doubt or a lack of competence among judges.[38] Today, there seems to be little controversy surrounding the disclosure of voting records in the Supreme Court.[39,40]

---

[38] The Supreme Court argued that if the citizens discern "weaknesses in human knowledge and expertise notably where they expect to find certitude, there is a risk that such an experience will diminish the high esteem in which the court was previously held before their insight was confined to the comprehensible outcome of the voting and deliberations." See parliamentary deliberations for August 1821, Part 5, Addendum, p. 128.

[39] Professor Peter Lødrup wrote in 1998: "Under today's perception of the law, public access to voting records is a matter of course, and it must be recognised that the Supreme Court's opposition was misguided." See Peter Lødrup (1998), "Høyesterett 1814–1996, noen historiske glimt (Norway's Supreme Court 1814–1996 – some historical glimpses)," in Stephan Tschudi-Madsen (ed.), *Norges Høyesterett (Norway's Supreme Court)*, Aschehoug, pp. 29–31.

[40] We find similar arguments in the debate between Deputy Governor at the Bank of England, Sir Ernest Harvey, and T. E. Gregory and J. M. Keynes, members of the so-called Macmillan committee. The following excerpts from the committee's report in 1931 is reported in Otmar Issing (2005), "Communication, Transparency, Accountability: Monetary Policy in the Twenty-First Century," *Federal Reserve Bank of St. Louis Review*, Vol. 87, No. 2, p. 73: "Committee member Gregory: 'I should like to ask you, Sir Ernest, whether you have ever considered the possibility of the Bank issuing an Annual Report on the lines of the Annual Report of the Federal Reserve

On Central Banking

Norges Bank is not only responsible for securing price stability, but also has a duty to promote stability in the banking system and financial markets. In principle, the same transparency considerations apply here, but with certain exceptions.[41]

Many of us were surprised and experienced associations with the interwar years when we saw television footage of depositors queuing at the doors of the crisis-hit British

Board, for instance?' Deputy Governor Harvey: 'I confess I am sometimes nervous at the thought of publication unless it is historical. The question is whether, when it is merely historical it is of any particular value, or whether from the fact that it is issued from the central bank undue importance may be attributed to certain things that are stated, more importance than perhaps they merit....' Committee member Keynes: 'Arising from Professor Gregory's questions, is it a practice of the Bank of England never to explain what its policy is?' Harvey: 'Well, I think it has been our practice to leave our actions to explain our policy.' Keynes: 'Or the reasons for its policy?' Harvey: 'It is a dangerous thing to start to give reasons.' Keynes: 'Or to defend itself against criticism?' Harvey: 'As regards criticism, I am afraid, though the Committee may not all agree, we do not admit there is need for defence; to defend ourselves is somewhat akin to a lady starting to defend her virtue.'"

[41] For a discussion of central bank transparency and financial stability, see for example Jakob De Haan and Sander Oosterloo (2006), "Transparency and Accountability of Central Banks in Their Role of Financial Stability Supervisor in OECD Countries," *European Journal of Law and Economics*, Vol. 22, No. 3, pp. 255–271.

bank Northern Rock in 2007. In a situation where a bank's solvency comes into doubt, depositors may rush to withdraw their cash. It is easy to conceive of a situation where a bank that is in fact solid, but has payment problems, might collapse if the authorities expose the problems to the general public. Moreover, banks may take excessive risks if they know the authorities will come to their rescue. It can be argued that in this case it may be appropriate for the central bank to engage in what is referred to in diplomatic parlance as "constructive ambiguity."[42,43]

Striking a balance between transparency and financial stability can be difficult, as former prime minister Abraham Berge discovered. During the banking crisis in 1923, Berge provided in secrecy a deposit of NOK 25 million to

---

[42] See E. Gerald Corrigan (1990), "Future Priorities in Banking and Finance," Remarks given before the 62nd Annual Mid-Winter Meeting of the New York State Bankers' Association, 25 January 1990. Published in Federal Reserve Bank of New York Quarterly Review/Winter 1989–1990, p. 7. See also p. 36 in "Norske finansmarkeder – pengepolitikk og finansiell stabilitet (Norwegian financial markets – monetary policy and financial stability)," Norges Bank Occasional Papers No. 34 (2004).

[43] The concept of "constructive ambiguity" refers to the deliberate use of ambiguous language in order to advance a political purpose. The concept has been particularly associated with Henry Kissinger, said to be the foremost exponent of constructive ambiguity as a negotiating tactic.

support Norway's fifth largest bank, Handelsbanken. The following year, Berge convinced the Storting to inject more capital into Handelsbanken, but failed to inform the Storting of the previous support. The secret deposit came to light after the government stepped down in 1924. The criticism that followed culminated in 1926 in an impeachment case against Berge and six of his ministers. A majority of the judges were of the opinion that the support provided in 1923 was punishable by law, but Berge and the ministers were nevertheless acquitted on the ground of the statute of limitations.[44,45]

The Art of Communication

Public disclosure of information is necessary, but not sufficient, for transparency. Communication is also important, but is a difficult art.

[44] See Riksrettstidende 1926/1927.

[45] On 7 November 2008, Bloomberg LP (on behalf of Bloomberg News) filed a federal lawsuit against the Federal Reserve for violation of the Freedom of Information Act. The news agency had called on the central bank to identify the U.S. banks funded by its emergency lending because the taxpayers should be aware of the risks involved in these investments. The Fed refused to name the borrowers or disclose the amounts of loans or the assets banks provided as collateral, arguing that doing so might "set off a run by depositors and unsettle shareholders." See article "Fed makes taxpayers 'involuntary investors' in banks, suit says," *Bloomberg*, 15 April 2009.

On Transparency

Good communication should satisfy three criteria.[46] First, the communication should be *clear*. The information should not be subject to misinterpretation and should not be so imprecise that it is not given weight. Central banks have not always been associated with clear and good communication. Alan Greenspan expressed this in the following statement: "Since becoming a central banker, I have learned to mumble with great incoherence. If I turn out to be particularly clear, you've probably misunderstood what I have said."[47]

Second, communication should be *effective*. It should not be time-consuming and demanding for the recipient to find and interpret the relevant information. It must be adapted to the target group.[48,49]

---

[46] See, for example, Bernhard Winkler (2000), "Which Kind of Transparency? On the Need for Clarity in Monetary Policy-Making," European Central Bank Working Paper No. 26.

[47] As cited in Petra M. Geraats (2007), "The Mystique of Central Bank Speak," *International Journal of Central Banking*, March, p. 37.

[48] Effective communication to market participants is particularly important. As economists with a university background, we often feel the need to build up a series of arguments and weigh various considerations before arriving at a conclusion. But this can sometimes render communication less effective. Financial market participants prefer to be presented with the conclusion first so that they can respond to it quickly.

[49] As part of its project to disseminate information about the central bank to various target groups, the Reserve Bank of India has made

The third criterion for good communication is that it must be *honest*. I referred earlier to the principle that the external communication should reflect the internal deliberations. It is an honest matter to communicate that decisions are difficult and often made on an uncertain basis. But it is just as important – and more challenging – to explain *why* it is difficult and which factors have been considered and given weight.

Before the rebuilding of Bislett Stadium in 2004, the organization Bislett Alliansen was to decide where the Bislett Games should be moved. The choice stood between Drammen and Bergen. They chose Bergen. The head of the organization said to the Norwegian news agency Norsk Telegrambyrå (NTB): "I have participated for almost twenty years, and this was the most difficult decision I have been involved in. At the end of the day, the decision was made on the basis of an overall assessment."[50] The way this was reported by the news agency did not make it easy to understand the actual background for the assessment.[51]

several comic strips for the benefit of school children. See www.rbi.org.in/financialeducation/Home.aspx.

[50] See article "Bergen fikk Bislett Games 2004 (The 2004 Bislett Games goes to Bergen)," *NTB*, 6 October 2003.

[51] A more detailed explanation was probably available but was not included in the media coverage.

I remember listening to this report on the radio while driving. It made me think about the formulations in our own press releases. To be honest, they were not much clearer. I saw room for improvement, and we have subsequently made efforts to improve the communication of our assessments. We have nevertheless experienced that it can be demanding to communicate why we arrive at one conclusion and not another.

Can We Become More Transparent?

Views on transparency and communication are constantly changing. As mentioned, Norges Bank has become more transparent in recent years. But is there room for even more transparency?

I readily admit that we were uncertain before taking new steps. When we first start publishing information, it is difficult to retreat. But the experience so far has been positive.[52] In some areas, therefore, I believe there is

[52] My predecessor as Deputy Governor, Jarle Bergo, delivered a speech a few years ago where he presented a mathematical equation that illustrated the assessments underlying our interest rate setting (see "Interest Rate Projections in Theory and Practice," speech at Sanderstølen, 27 January 2007). I remember that we were uncertain about the reactions to this. My Swedish colleague Lars Svensson had recommended that such a target function be

room for increased transparency. Some observers have argued that Norges Bank and other central banks should provide information to the public about the models we use and how we use them.[53] I agree with this. It is difficult from a pedagogical viewpoint to explain how the models are used as a basis for economic policy. Because models are rough simplifications of reality, we must exercise considerable judgment when we use them. This is not always easy to document and explain. But, even

published in the interest of transparency, but no central bank had ever done this before. There was no first-page news of the type "this equation determines the interest rate." Our "bold step" proved to be fairly undramatic. It would seem that this is really the rule rather than the exception every time we have moved toward greater transparency. Bergo's lecture was included in the curriculum of economics professor Michael Woodford of Columbia University in New York.

[53] Norges Bank Watch 2008 writes: "Norges Bank should facilitate a more open discussion regarding the empirical performance of their (mechanical) forecasting models by communicating the role played by the 'judgment component' more clearly. This may encourage exploitation of the cumulative learning process in the scientific community as a whole, by which existing empirical models are improved or (eventually) overtaken by new and better ones." See Steinar Juel, Krisztina Molnaad, and Knut Røed (2008), "An Independent Review of Monetary Policymaking in Norway," Centre for Monetary Economics BI, p. 44.

though it may be difficult, it is not impossible and our aim is to improve in this area.

The management of the Government Pension Fund – Global is another activity of Norges Bank where transparency is important. Among the world's sovereign pension funds, Norway's is one of the most transparent. International organizations refer to it as an example of best practice. In Norway, the Fund has been both applauded and criticized for its communication. The Fund's annual report was one among six others nominated for the Farmand award for best annual report and website. However, the same report was also strongly criticized by the Norwegian journalist Per Egil Hegge for its impenetrable language.[54]

We are working toward improving our communication of the Fund's activity. The Fund's ultimate owners are the Norwegian people and we must improve the communication of the main management principles to that target group. We are making continuous efforts to improve our quarterly reports and our annual report. We are also

---

[54] Per Egil Hegge noted in particular the following sentence in the annual report: "The expected tracking error increased more than the absolute market volatility, primarily reflecting a closer correlation between returns from the different investment strategies." See Hegge's column in *Aftenposten*, 16 April 2009.

working to improve the Fund's website, which will include a continuous update of the Fund's value.

Conclusion

Transparency is important. Transparency contributes to strengthening confidence, and confidence is crucial for an effective monetary policy in normal times, but perhaps particularly in times of crisis. According to Lars Weisæth and Ragnar Kjeserud, two authorities in the field of crisis psychiatry, to be successful in managing a crisis, the responsible authorities must be perceived as competent and at the same time have a reputation for openness and honesty.[55]

I started this lecture by describing how the Bank of England managed the crisis during the 1780 Gordon riots. A military defense was necessary to safeguard society's values. The event gave rise to the expression "as safe as the Bank of England" and later "as safe as the bank."

We have experienced a deep financial crisis. We are now hopeful that it is coming to an end. The reputation of

---

[55] Lars Weisæth and Ragnar Kjeserud (2007), *Ledelse ved kriser: en praktisk veileder* (*Management during crises: a practical guide*), Gyldendal Akademisk, p. 71 (Norwegian only).

private banks has not been left untarnished. Banks' own behavior was one of the causes of the crisis. The very depth of the banking crisis is attributable to a collapse of trust among banks. They no longer considered their fellow banks as "safe." Financial markets stopped functioning. The expression "as safe as the bank" became somewhat hollow.

We have seen that the most unexpected places, such as small coastal towns and the northern region of Norway, have been hard hit by the financial crisis. The crisis has also left its mark on our language. In a tribute published in the newspaper Troms Folkeblad on the occasion of the fiftieth birthday of the manager of Troms soccer league, he is described as "as safe as Norges Bank" in his handling of protests and violations.[56] With that, the expression was brought back to its original source. And perhaps that means that Norges Bank's reputation has survived the financial crisis – at least in Troms!

When the Bank of England came under attack, many citizens had already volunteered as soldiers to defend the bank. They were outnumbered, but the very sight of them probably demoralized the mobs and led to their defeat.

---

[56] See article "Mr. Fotballkretsen fyller 50! (Mr. Soccer League turns 50)," *Troms Folkeblad*, 6 October 2009 (Norwegian only).

On Central Banking

Expectations and confidence were as important then as now. But there is a significant difference – that can summarize today's lecture. While central banks at that time upheld the value of money with walls and thundering muskets, today the value of money is safeguarded by confidence rooted in disclosure and transparency.

— ✣ CHAPTER THREE ✣ —

On Making Good Decisions

Introduction

When Hans Rasmus Astrup was appointed minister in Johan Sverdrup's government in 1885, he sold his business in Stockholm and moved back to Norway.[*] As I mentioned in my lecture here two years ago,[1] Astrup

[*] I would like to thank Øyvind Eitrheim, Amund Holmsen, Marie Norum Lerbak, Kjetil Olsen and Øistein Røisland for their valuable assistance in preparing this lecture. I would also like to thank Helle Snellingen for her contribution to the translation of the Norwegian text into English.
[1] The lecture "On Keeping Promises," commentaries by Endre Stavang and Henrik Syse, and Francis Sejersted's summary of the debate are published in Norges Bank Occasional Paper

was at the time perhaps Norway's wealthiest man. On his return to Norway, he needed a place to live, bought a plot of land here in Drammensveien, and decided to build the house we are sitting in now.

The question might be raised whether it was a good decision to build such a large and ostentatious house. But Astrup was not just looking for a home for his family. The house was also intended to provide a venue for interdisciplinary and political discussions.[2]

We all make many decisions every single day, some more important than others. And we all presumably want these decisions to be good ones. But how can we ensure that a decision is good? This is a weighty and far-reaching question. If I am to make meaningful contribution, I will need to limit my focus.

Norges Bank makes many decisions. The monetary policy decisions every six weeks are awaited with particular interest. Based on my experience from interest rate decision making, I will focus on how the quality of a decision can be assessed. Even though I am speaking

---

No. 39 (2009): www.norges-bank.no/Upload/75326/39_On_keep ing_promises.pdf.

[2] Kim Gunnar Helsvig (2007), *Elitisme på norsk. Det Norske Videnskaps- Akademi 1945–2007 [Elitism in Norway. The Norwegian Academy of Science and Letters 1945–2007]*, Oslo: Novus forlag, pp. 18–19.

from my own perspective, I hope I am able to touch on more general issues that are of wider relevance.

Independence Provides a Sound Framework for Interest Rate Decisions

Most countries have now delegated the task of ensuring price stability to the central bank. This is also the case in Norway. The government has set an inflation target for monetary policy and delegated the operational conduct of monetary policy to Norges Bank.[3]

This framework can be regarded as an institutional solution to the problem of avoiding major mistakes. An independent central bank is better able to give priority to long-term interests over short-term gains.

That it is tempting, but dangerous, for a government to focus on short-term gains was a lesson Greek politicians learned in 2010. Government spending exceeded revenues over a long period. Accounts and official statistics were fudged. Politicians may have hoped to secure a quick admission for Greece into the euro area, with the advantages this would bring. They may have also believed that

---

[3] See inter alia Report No. 29 (2000–2001) to the Storting, Guidelines for Economic Policy, Ministry of Finance, and the Regulation on Monetary Policy of 29 March 2001.

high government spending and low taxes might help their reelection prospects. Instead, they now have to steer the country through harsh reforms and substantial cuts.[4]

The Norwegian economist Finn Kydland received the Nobel Prize for economics in 2004 for having shown that on the whole, monetary policy decisions are better if policy makers delegate interest rate setting to an independent central bank under a clear mandate.[5] As a central bank we must adhere to the mandate we have been given and be able to set the key rate based on a professional assessment.[6] This is a system that lays a solid foundation for making good decisions.

[4] The euro area operates under rules intended in principle to facilitate long-term policy choices. The Maastricht criteria require participating states to keep fiscal deficits and public debt within defined limits. Recent history has shown that this framework must be reinforced through sanctions. Decision-makers need an incentive to comply with the rules in practice.

[5] See Finn E. Kydland and Edward C. Prescott (1977), "Rules Rather than Discretion: The Inconsistency of Optimal Plans," *Journal of Political Economy*, Vol. 85, No. 3, pp. 473–491.

[6] See Arne Kloster and Kristin Solberg-Johansen (2006), "Forecasting in Norges Bank," *Economic Bulletin*, 3/2006; Jarle Bergo (2007), "Interest rate projections in theory and practice," speech at the Foreign Exchange Seminar of Norwegian Economists, 26 January, available at www.norges-bank.no/no/om/publisert/foredrag-og-taler/ 2007/speech-2007-01-26/; and Svein Gjedrem (2004), "Inflation targeting – some theory with main focus on practice," speech at the Centre of Monetary Economics/Norwegian School of Management,

We Make Decisions under Uncertainty

Independence alone does not guarantee good decisions. Even if an independent central bank is better positioned to avoid having short-term expediency and changing preferences dictate interest rate policy, its decisions must be made under considerable uncertainty.

We have imperfect knowledge about the state of the economy, and we are not absolutely certain of how economic relationships function. Alan Greenspan, the former Chairman of the U.S. Federal Reserve, described this in the following words:"Uncertainty is not just an important feature of the monetary policy landscape; it is the defining characteristic of that landscape."[7] Sometimes, the nature of the uncertainty allows one to draw inferences regarding the probabilities of different outcomes. It is possible, in other words, to judge the risks one is facing, at least to a certain degree. In that case, decisions can be made on the basis of a calculated risk, which is an approach underlying theories of equity investment,[8] for example.

8 June, available at www.norges-bank.no/en/om/publisert/fore drag-og-taler/2004/2004-06-08/.

[7] In Alan Greenspan's opening remarks to the Jackson Hole symposium in 2003, available at www.bis.org/review/r030905a.pdf.

[8] See, for example, William F. Sharpe (1964), "Capital Asset Prices: A Theory of Market Equilibrium under Conditions of Risk," *Journal*

But the financial crisis reminded us that keeping the overall risk picture in view may be difficult. When Queen Elizabeth visited the London School of Economics in autumn 2008 she asked why no one had foreseen the crisis. The British Academy Forum replied to the Queen in a letter six months later. Included in the letter was the following: "One of our major banks, now mainly in public ownership, reputedly had 4,000 risk managers. But the difficulty was seeing the risk to the system as a whole rather than to any specific financial instrument or loan.... They frequently lost sight of the bigger picture."[9] In setting the key policy rate, too, we often face more fundamental uncertainty, where it is very difficult to calculate probabilities for possible scenarios.[10] In decision situations like these, it may be appropriate to establish routines that can guard against especially severe consequences.

Many might believe that since Norges Bank's key policy rate is set every six weeks, there might be scope for correction should it transpire that economic

---

of Finance, Vol. 19, No. 3; and Harry M. Markowitz (1952), "Portfolio Selection," Journal of Finance, Vol. 12, No. 1.

[9] The letter from the British Academy to the Queen is available at http://media.ft.com/cms/3e3b6ca8-7a08-11de-b86f-00144feabdc0.pdf.

[10] See Frank H. Knight (1921), Risk, Uncertainty, and Profit, Boston: Houghton Mifflin.

developments were not as expected. To a certain extent this is the case. But since it takes time for the effects of our decisions to come into evidence, our scope for correction is in reality rather narrow. Setting the key rate at an inappropriate level for a period of time may have serious consequences for the Norwegian economy.

Without complete and reliable information at our disposal, it is easy to err. A number of studies have shown that in such situations humans often resort to more or less qualified guesses, gut feelings, or rules of thumb.

Allow me to offer an example involving distance judgment. Ordinarily, the closer an object is, the more clearly we will see it. Thus, if they see an object clearly, most people will perceive it as nearby. But when the astronauts landed on the moon, they had great difficulty judging distances, almost always underestimating them. The reason was that visibility was unusually clear and they were in a landscape without known references.[11]

One approach to uncertainty is to do what others do in similar circumstances. The United Kingdom decided to

---

[11] See the article "Fotspor med historie (Footsteps with history)," *Aftenposten*, 8 July 1989, and Rod Pyle (2007), *Destination Moon: The Apollo Missions in the Astronauts' Own Words*, Harper Paperbacks. For further discussion and additional examples, see Thomas Gilovich, Dale Griffin, and Daniel Kahneman (2002), *Heuristics and Biases: The Psychology of Intuitive Judgment*, Cambridge University Press.

abandon the gold standard in summer 1931. In practice this meant a devaluation of the pound sterling against the U.S. dollar. A few days later, Norway and the other Nordic countries decided to follow suit. History has shown that the countries that devalued in 1931 weathered the depression better than those that did not.[12] Following the British lead was a decision that produced a good outcome.

In 1949 there was a new sterling devaluation, this time 30 percent against the U.S. dollar. As in 1931, the Norwegian government announced that the value of the krone would be lowered correspondingly.[13] But unlike at

---

[12] See the discussion in Tore Jørgen Hanisch, Espen Søilen, and Gunhild Ecklund (1999), *Norsk økonomisk politikk i det 20. århundre. Verdivalg i en åpen økonomi, [Norwegian economic history in the 20th century. Ethical choices in an open economy]*, Høyskoleforlaget, Kristiansand.

[13] The government had discussed how Norway should respond to a British devaluation. However, they had not reached a final conclusion and the government was split. The Minister of Trade and Industry at the time, Erik Brofoss, advocated following the United Kingdom's actions to the full, and was supported in this view by Gunnar Jahn, the governor of Norges Bank. They feared a substantial loss of competitiveness if Norway was the only one among its trading partners not to follow the sterling devaluation. When the magnitude of the U.K. devaluation became known, Gunnar Jahn was attending the annual meeting of the IMF in Washington, D.C. He had received provisional authorization from the government to

that time, the level of activity in Norway was now high, and demand pressures were elevated. The krone devaluation triggered high inflation.[14] This time, the rule

> inform the IMF that Norway would follow a moderate British devaluation. The expectation was a sterling devaluation of around 20 percent. However, Erik Brofoss had informed Jahn that he favored following the U.K. move regardless of how much they devalued. At an IMF dinner on the evening of 16 September Jahn received a business card with the date "18 September," the number "30.5," and the words "Tell Bramsnæs" written on it (Bramsnæs was the director of Danmarks Nationalbank, who was also attending the IMF meeting). The business card revealed the date and magnitude of the British devaluation. It was a busy night. Jahn sent a telegram to Brofoss where he recommended that Norway devalue the krone to the same extent as the United Kingdom. By then the Ministry of Trade and Industry had already been informed of the United Kingdom's decision through official channels. Then, without first consulting with the other members of the government, Brofoss decided that the Norwegian krone should be devalued by 30.5 percent. After being instructed by Brofoss, Gunnar Jahn informed the IMF of the decision on behalf of the Norwegian government in a letter dated 17 September. See Gunhild J. Ecklund (2008), "Creating a New Role for an Old Central Bank: The Bank of Norway 1945–1954," Series of Dissertations 2/2008, BI Norwegian School of Management, pp. 141–143, and William Jansen (1975), "Devalueringen i 1949 (The devaluation of 1949)," thesis, NTNU, Trondheim.

[14] For more on the background for these decisions, see Gunnar Jahn, Alf Eriksen, and Preben Munthe (1966), *Norges Bank gjennom 150 år (Norges Bank through 150 years)*, Oslo: Norges Bank; and Nicolai

"do what the United Kingdom does" contributed to a less favorable outcome.[15]

Groups Often Make Better Decisions than Individuals

What steps can we take to ensure that important decisions are the best they can be, even if they have to be made under uncertainty?

In his novel *L*, Erlend Loe discusses advantages and drawbacks of different decision systems. The author-narrator has embarked on an expedition to a South Pacific island with six companions. On the island they

Rygg (1950), *Norges Bank i mellomkrigstiden (Norges Bank in the interwar period)*, Oslo: Gyldendal Norsk Forlag.

[15] In 1965 the former director of Statistics Norway, Odd Aukrust, assessed the successes and mistakes in Norwegian economic policy since the Second World War. Concerning the devaluation decision in 1949, he wrote: "This devaluation was probably the most important single economic decision made in this country since 1945, with a greater impact on prices and income distribution than any wage settlement. There can hardly be any doubt that in the 1950s, price changes would have been less abrupt in Norway if the devaluation had not taken place." See Odd Aukrust (1965), *Tjue års økonomisk politikk i Norge: suksesser og mistak (Twenty years of economic policy in Norway: successes and mistakes)*, Articles from Statistics Norway, no. 15.

experiment with different forms of social organization. After the group tries despotism, anarchy, democracy, and so on, Loe concludes that enlightened despotism has much to recommend it: "Of course it very much depends on who the ruler is and how enlightened he or she is, but at its best this is probably one of the more sensible forms of government."[16] Martin, one of the other members of the expedition, also thinks that this system might work well. He stresses, however, that the form of despotism must be a truly enlightened one: "Not just moderately enlightened, but ultra-enlightened. The ruler needs to be highly educated, plus be well travelled and have lots and lots of varied interests.... Just find an exceedingly likeable individual, someone you trust, someone who is warm-hearted and good-natured, and ask him or her to manage things as best they can."[17] Most people would probably argue that despite certain benefits, enlightened despotism would not be very robust. As you may have noted, a number of assumptions underlie Martin's conclusion, and these assumptions are not always satisfied. Delegating decision-making responsibility to a group may help to guard against situations where the individual's

---

[16] Erlend Loe (1999), *L*, J. W. Cappelens forlag, p. 376.
[17] Loe (1999), pp. 397–398.

weaknesses and vested interests come to dominate. It can also provide some insurance against serious missteps, which seems to be particularly important when decisions are made under uncertainty.

This notion is part of the justification for the jury system in our courts of law. The French philosopher Marquis de Condorcet's now well-known jury theorem states that the higher the number of members of the group is, the higher the probability is that the group will make the correct decision by majority vote.[18] Group decision making has been widely accepted, not only by the courts but also by businesses, public administration, and elected governing bodies.

In his book *The Wisdom of Crowds*, James Surowiecki cites a number of examples where large groups outperform individuals or small groups of experts. Contestants on the television game show *Who Wants to Be a Millionaire?* have various so-called "lifelines," including telephoning a smart friend or asking the studio audience for help. It has transpired that the studio audience is the contestants' absolute best bet. The majority of the studio audience votes for the correct answer nine out of

---

[18] This outcome assumes that each member of the group singly is more likely to arrive at the correct conclusion than the wrong one.

ten times, beating out smart friends, who provide the correct answer only 65 percent of the time.[19]

This decision-making strategy, where each individual in a group gives an answer independently of the others, can function well for some types of decisions. But there may also be advantages to allowing the group to arrive at a decision through deliberation.

The economists Alan S. Blinder and John Morgan have shown in several experiments that students who work together to solve a problem obtain a better result than the average of the students who work alone.[20] In Blinder's words, "the group seems to foster some sort of collective

---

[19] See James Surowiecki (2004), *The Wisdom of Crowds*, London: Little, Brown, pp. 3–4. This example was also cited in the speech "Uncertainty in macroeconomic policy making: art or science?," which Mervyn King, Governor of the Bank of England, gave on 22 March 2010, and is available at www.bankofengland.co.uk/publications/news/2010/034.htm. That we both use this example may not be a coincidence. I received my copy of *The Wisdom of Crowds* from Dr. John Llewellyn. Llewellyn and King were fellow students at Cambridge.

[20] See Alan S. Blinder and John Morgan (2005), "Are Two Heads Better Than One: An Experimental Analysis of Group versus Individual Decision Making," *Journal of Money, Credit and Banking*, Vol. 37, No. 5, pp. 789–811; and Alan S. Blinder and John Morgan (2007), "Leadership in Groups: A Monetary Policy Experiment," CEPS Working Paper No. 151.

wisdom that makes the whole (a bit) greater than the sum of its parts."[21] These experiments indicate that there may be benefits to be gained from group interaction, which can provide increased access to varied knowledge, can deconstruct opinions, and can test viewpoints. We can learn from each other.

I have learned a lot in this area from the organizational psychologist Ingeborg Baustad and her colleagues. Baustad argues that there may be a relationship between intragroup communication and task solving. Some tasks are so simple that unilateral communication is sufficient. For deliberative tasks the requirements are higher. Active bilateral communication is necessary, with a willingness to listen to the views of the others in the group. For more strategic decision making, the level of communication must be raised a notch further. The hallmarks of such a high communication level are curiosity about the other person's views and the ability to broaden one's views or change one's mind as a result of discussion with others. This type of communication normally requires a high level of professional competence, mutual sympathy and trust, and

---

[21] Alan S. Blinder (2008), "On the Design of Monetary Policy Committees," Norges Bank Working Paper, 2008/6.

a large degree of openness. The potential reward is better decisions by the group.[22]

As in most central banks, interest rate decisions in Norges Bank are entrusted to a committee. Committee deliberations are informed by advice given by the governor and deputy governor of Norges Bank. Norges Bank's Executive Board has seven members. The number of committee members at other central banks varies between three and twenty-two.[23] A committee of many members can draw on an ample supply of varied backgrounds and opinions, but a larger number will then also have to have a say in the final decision. While research has yet to determine the optimal committee size, Anne Sibert, one of the experts in this field, has said that the committee should be "dinner size."[24]

---

[22] See more about this in Erling S. Andersen, Ingeborg Baustad, and Åge Sørsveen (1994), *Ledelse på norsk [Norwegian management]*, Oslo: Ad Notam Gyldendal, pp. 117–126.

[23] Three in Switzerland and twenty-two in the European Central Bank.

[24] See more about this in, for example, Alan S. Blinder (2008) and Anne Sibert (2006), "Central Banking by Committee," *International Finance*, Vol. 9, No. 2, pp. 145–168. In September 2007 Norges Bank hosted a conference on monetary policy committees. The opening address was given by Alan S. Blinder, former vice chairman of the Federal Reserve Board, and one of the economists who

But Groups Are No Guarantee for Good Decisions

Norges Bank's Executive Board can be described as a collegial committee. The committee seeks consensus through deliberations and its members stand behind the final decision.

The deliberative process does not necessarily lead to a better decision. When the group members share the same world view and thinking, groupthink can lead the members astray. There is typically little dissent in discussions where participants think similarly. The group can therefore be convinced that their common standpoint must be right.[25]

Nor is it unusual for independent thinking to be lost in a group setting. At an internal conference, the research

has focused most on group decision making. Anne Sibert also attended this conference.

[25] It has also been shown that when people are in groups of like-minded persons, and especially when they are socially isolated, they are prone to taking more extreme positions than they would on their own. The psychologist Irving L. Janis is particularly known for his research into groupthink. His analyses concerned U.S. foreign policy, where groupthink might deserve much of the blame for competent persons making poor decisions. See Irving L. Janis (1972), *Victims of Groupthink: A Psychological Study of Foreign-Policy Decisions and Fiascoes*, Boston: Houghton Mifflin Company.

department at Norges Bank was divided into three groups tasked with answering three sets of questions. Unbeknownst to the other participants, one member in each group had been instructed to argue for the wrong answer within one of the question sets. They did their job well. The groups did very poorly on the set of questions where the conference organizer's confederates argued for the wrong answer.[26]

There is thus a danger that members of a group can be swayed by other members to make the wrong choice. But falling into the opposite trap – paying insufficient heed to others' advice – is not unusual either. This is a pitfall that many people who have been in management for a while will be acquainted with. Psychologists have known that such exaggerated self-confidence is found in many occupations.[27] There is no reason to believe

---

[26] The psychologist Salomon Asch conducted a number of similar experiments in the 1950s. He found that "the tendency to conformity in our society is so strong that reasonably intelligent and well meaning young people are willing to call black white." See Salomon E. Asch (1995), "Opinions and Social Pressure," *Scientific American*, Vol. 193, No. 5, pp. 31–35.

[27] See overview and further references in Carl Andreas Claussen, Egil Matsen, Øistein Røisland, and Ragnar Torvik (2009), "Overconfidence, Monetary Policy Committees and Chairman Dominance," Norges Bank Working Paper, 2009/17.

that we economists are so different from others in that regard.

Norges Bank's Executive Board consists of five external members with varied backgrounds, in addition to the governor and deputy governor of the Bank. The external members have influence over decisions on a par with the internal members. The Bank is in a peculiar situation in that the central bank governor is both administrative head of the Bank and chairman of the Executive Board. The external members are not full-time employees of Norges Bank, and their primary occupations are outside the central bank. In this respect, the Executive Board has an important control function. Its external members can act as a counterweight to any internal cultures of opinion that may arise at the Bank.[28]

---

[28] The members of the Executive Board are appointed by the government. According to Proposition No. 81 (2002–2003) to the Odelsting, the appointment process shall ensure that the Executive Board reflects a broad range of backgrounds and expertise, with particular emphasis on economics and finance, as well as a thorough understanding of economic issues. The proposition states that the Executive Board shall be composed of persons of different backgrounds to ensure that it is capable of being critical of its own assessments. See Proposition No. 81 (2002–2003) to the Odelsting: Om lov om endringer i sentralbankloven og finansieringsvirksomhetsloven og om opphevelse av valutareguleringsloven og penge- og kredittreguleringsloven (Concerning an Act to amend the Norges Bank Act and

On Making Good Decisions

In some central banks, such as Sveriges Riksbank and the Bank of England, interest rate decisions are made by individualistic committees. Decisions are made by majority voting, with each member individually accountable for his or her vote. There are advantages and drawbacks to both individualistic and collegial committees. As I discussed in last year's lecture, individual accountability can provide good incentives. There is no one to hide behind. At the same time such accountability entails more work and probably full-time employment at the Bank. In that case, the former outsiders may quickly

the Financial Institutions Act and concerning the repeal of the Exchange Control Act and the Monetary and Credit Policy Act). Ministry of Finance Board appointment guidelines and rules relating to limitations on members' ownership interests and functions are set out in the Norges Bank Act and the Regulation of 7 August 2000 relating to Norges Bank's Executive Board members' relationship to other credit institutions and undertakings. Executive Board members cannot inter alia be married to a member of parliament and external members cannot receive remuneration from or sit on the board or supervisory council of financial institutions, securities firms, or collective investment undertakings. Nor are they permitted to buy or sell fixed income or foreign exchange products when they are in possession of information concerning conditions that may influence prices, unless the information is available to the public. In addition, the general impartiality provisions under Section 6 of the Public Administration Act apply.

assimilate the internal culture. The control function of the external members might be lost.

How Do We Arrive at a Decision?

We also need to think carefully about how we should agree on a decision. There two approaches: premise-based or conclusion-based.[29]

The two approaches may have different outcomes. Allow me to offer a stylized example. Assume that a three-member committee is to reach an interest rate decision. The members base their decisions on two premises: inflation and pressures in the economy. The first member believes that inflation has risen more than expected, but finds that the pressures in the economy are broadly as expected. The interest rate should therefore be raised. The second member believes that inflation is broadly as expected, but the pressures in the economy are surprisingly high on the upside. This member, too, will conclude, that the interest rate should be adjusted upward. The third member believes that developments have been

---

[29] For a discussion of the relationship between conclusion-based and premise-based decisions, see Carl Andreas Claussen and Øistein Røisland (2010), "A Auantitative Discursive Dilemma," *Social Choice and Welfare*, Vol. 35, No. 1.

as expected and concludes that the key rate should remain unchanged.

In a conclusion-based decision, the majority would vote to increase the key rate. Two out of three members came to this conclusion. But a premise-based conclusion would in this case have produced a different outcome. Two out of the three members believed that inflation and economic pressures were as expected. A premise-based decision would thus leave the key rate unchanged.

Many will favor the premise-based approach because it gives weight to the underlying basis for the decisions we make.[30] Research has also shown that it is better to discuss and vote on the grounds for any disagreements than to go directly to the conclusion.[31] At Norges Bank we base our procedures on a premise-based decision-making process.

---

[30] See, for example, Bruce Chapman (2003), "Rational Choice and Categorical Reason," *University of Pennsylvania Law Review*, Vol. 151, No. 3, pp. 1169–1210; and Philip Pettit (2001), "Deliberative Democracy and the Discursive Dilemma," *Philosophical Issues* (supplement to *Noûs*), Vol. 11, pp. 268–299.

[31] See the discussion in Carl Andreas Claussen and Øistein Røisland (2010), "The Discursive Dilemma in Monetary Policy," Norges Bank Working Paper, 2010/5. It should be noted that premise-based decisions can be vulnerable to strategic behavior. It is possible to vote on the premises in such a way as to reach a preferred outcome.

On Central Banking

Economists working at Norges Bank have an important role in decision making, particularly because decisions are premise-based.[32] The Bank's economists thus constitute a stabilizing element in the decision-making process that is robust to changes in central bank management and the Executive Board's external members.

For the Bank's economists to perform this role properly, it is essential that they are of a very high professional calibre. Here the Executive Board also performs a vital role, providing constant feedback on the quality of the research supporting policy decisions. The Board also discusses the Bank's personnel policy and measures to maintain and develop the skills of staff economists.

But Norges Bank has a monopoly on setting the key interest rate in Norway. One of the dangers of monopolies is a tendency toward complacency, which is why it is imperative to be in the critical spotlight. This keeps us, Board and staff economists alike, constantly on our toes and helps us to develop as professionals. This, in turn, results in better decisions.

Every year we must stand to account for the way in which we carry out our mandate. There is reporting to

---

[32] The material on which interest rate decisions is based is published on the Norges Bank website. For a more detailed discussion, see "On Transparency" in Norges Bank Occasional Paper No. 41 (2010).

the government and hearings in the Storting. In addition, the Ministry of Finance commissions an independent review of monetary policy though what is known as "Norges Bank Watch."[33] At the same time we are open about what we do and why. There are external evaluations of work routines and professional standards.[34] There are no comparable institutions in Norway – there is only one central bank. The benchmark must be international best practice. The evaluations are generally performed by international central banking experts or economists at other central banks.

Was the Decision Good?

Even if our delegating authority and critics have access to the background for our decisions and the way we arrive

---

[33] Reports from Norges Bank Watch are available at www.bi.no/en/ Research/Research-Centres/Centre-for-Monetary-Economics-CME/Norges-Bank-Watch.

[34] See inter alia David Longworth and Asbjørn Rødseth (2003), "Report on the Decision-Making Process and the Strategy Document"; Hans Genberg, Charles Wyplosz, and Andrea Fracasso (2003), "How Do Central Banks Write? An Evaluation of Inflation Targeting Central Banks"; and Ingimundur Fridriksson (2010), "The Monetary Policy Report Process in Norges Bank," all available at www.norges-bank.no/en/about/published/publications/external-reports.

at them, one big question still remains: What should the criteria be for judging whether our decisions are good?

The objective of monetary policy is a natural place at which to begin our assessment. Have we or have we not achieved price stability? Even if we make our best efforts, there is no guarantee that we will succeed in reaching this objective. The key policy rate is not the only factor affecting the economy and that can disturb the outcome. Even so, we can give weight to accurate information, assess the most relevant alternatives, and listen to input. Making a decision on this basis might excuse us from blame if the outcome should in retrospect turn out to be unfavorable.[35]

---

[35] A fundamental principle of criminal law is that a person can only be judged if that person can be charged with a criminal offence and is proven guilty. There are two forms of guilt: One is guilty with intent, which typically means that the offender intended to produce the negative outcome. The other form of guilt is negligence, which somewhat simplified implies a failure to use reasonable care or prudence. In determining whether an offender has acted with negligence, his or her behavior must be measured against ordinary reasonable and prudent behavior in a comparable situation. A Supreme Court ruling from 1984 provides an illustration of negligence consideration. The Supreme Court was to decide whether the driver of a car was negligent when in a very difficult intersection he crashed into a car that had the right of way on the other crossing road. The collision occurred in the midst of rush

Let us return to the decision in 1949 to follow the pound sterling. As I said, in retrospect the consequences of this decision appear to be less favorable. Nor, perhaps, was the decision-making process sufficiently thorough. Doubts have been raised as to whether alternative courses of action were adequately assessed.[36]

But the authorities apparently felt that they had no choice other than a comparable devaluation of the krone.[37] Norway's competitiveness could have been weakened

---

traffic, and the Court argued that crossing traffic should be expected at that time. However, a number of conditions made it difficult for the man to see the traffic before he was close to the intersection. It was dark, with rain and sleet and icy roads. On the other hand, the driver was very familiar with the site and he should have been aware of the all the risks at the intersection. As he did not adjust his driving so that he was able to stop, the Court found that the driver had acted negligently. See Norsk Retstidende (Norwegian journal of law) 1984–1991.

[36] Preben Munthe, professor of economics, believes that the government was probably surprised by the magnitude of the sterling devaluation. He writes: "When the authorities learned of the British decision, they probably felt they were under time pressure, which is why the situation was not nearly as thoroughly discussed as it actually could have been." See Jahn, Eriksen, and Munthe (1966), p. 371.

[37] Nor was this decision criticised by the business sector or the press, and in its publication "Økonomiske utsyn over året 1949," Statistics Norway wrote that "the Norwegian external economy is so closely

substantially if they had not followed the British move. In view of this, it can therefore be argued that their motives for doing what they did were good ones.

The 1949 decision also illustrates the problem of counterfactual analyses. Determining what might have happened if the authorities had acted otherwise is no easy task. Allow me to present a hypothetical example: The central bank thinks financial imbalances are building up, and the Executive Board sets the key rate higher than it otherwise would have done. While a financial crisis does not actually materialize, unemployment rises and economic growth slows. Inflation could fall below target. In this situation, it may be difficult to assess whether the Board made a good decision to raise the key rate.

Such assessments of motives and outcomes are also the subject of moral philosophy and its discussion of what constitutes a good decision. In setting the key rate, both intentionalist and deontological ethics will provide us with the same guidance as to what good decisions are. In both cases, the decision must be based on achieving the objective of monetary policy, and that alone. From a

linked to that of the United Kingdom, that there was hardly any alternative to following the pound sterling." See Jahn, Eriksen, and Munthe (1966), p. 371.

consequentialist standpoint, it matters little whether the intentions were good, if the consequences of the decision were not. Our decisions are good only if we reach the objective of price stability. As mentioned, our performance cannot be measured by whether inflation is always at target, partly because the economy is frequently exposed to abrupt and unexpected shocks. We will nearly always be slightly over or slightly under the target. But over time we can expect that these disturbances will even out, and in the long run we must also be evaluated on whether or not we achieve the objective of monetary policy. Have we, or have we not, achieved price stability these past ten years?

Conclusion

Making a good decision is of little use unless one also manages to have it implemented. Norges Bank enjoys a privileged position. When we make a decision, we can also implement it. Our independence gives us the freedom to decide what the key policy rate shall be.

In other areas of society, it is not always the case that those who are qualified to make good decisions also have the power to implement them. In the interest of democratic governance there may be good reasons why this is so, but the decision-making process will then require considerable attention.

We can concentrate on promoting an understanding of the decisions we make. We must be transparent about what we do, and explain premises, economic relationships, and results. Our decisions must be well communicated and understood. If we are unsuccessful in this respect, our reputation may be impaired.

Independence, transparency, and good decisions are intertwined. Independence is a precondition for keeping promises. Keeping promises was the topic of my lecture here two years ago.[38] We must also communicate and explain interest rate decisions to the public so that they have confidence that we are discharging our duties properly. Transparency is a precondition for accountability and that was the topic of my lecture here last year.[39] Today I have been speaking about how we can arrive at decisions that are good ones. Adequate institutional arrangements, high-quality professionals, and appropriate routines are important elements for doing just that.

---

[38] See Norges Bank Occasional Paper No. 39 (2009).

[39] The lecture "On Transparency"; the commentaries by Inge Lorange Backer, Andreas Føllesdal, and Bernt Aardal; and Aanund Hylland's summary of the debate are published in Norges Bank Occasional Paper No. 41 (2010): www.norges-bank.no/Upload/81531/On_transparency_occ_paper_41.pdf.

Hans Rasmus Astrup died in 1898, twelve years after this building was completed. Astrup's two daughters sold the house to the Norwegian Academy of Science and Letters a few years after their father's passing. They gave the Academy a gift of 106,000 kroner to go toward buying the house. The remaining funds were raised from donations.[40]

Was the decision to build this stately residence a good one? Yes; given the outcome, it must be said to have been a very good decision indeed. Ever since Astrup's time, Drammensveien 78 has been a venue for interdisciplinary discussions. The benefits of learning across disciplines are well illustrated by the success of Olympiatoppen. Olympiatoppen serves as a venue for different sports. Where coaches and leaders have traditionally focused on international developments in their own disciplines, Olympiatoppen also gives them an opportunity to learn from one another's experiences, across disciplines. Many believe that this is part of the reason for Norway's numerous Olympic medals in recent decades.[41]

For 150 years the Norwegian Academy of Science and Letters, by fostering contact across academic disciplines,

---

[40] See Helsvig (2007), pp. 19–20, footnote 2.

[41] See the article "Særnorsk oppskrift for OL-gull (Uniquely Norwegian recipe for Olympic gold)," 10 February 2010, available at (in Norwegian) www.forskning.no/artikler/2010/februar/242243.

has functioned as a kind of Olympiatoppen for science and scholarship. The Academy has always convened its members for discussions of topics that, although maybe rooted in a single field, are at the same time broader in scope and of common interest.[42] This lays the foundation for making good decisions.

[42] See Øyvind Østerud's introduction in the Norwegian Academy of Science and Letters annual report for 2009 at (in Norwegian) www.dnva.no/c26776/liste.html?tid=26997.

CHAPTER FOUR

On Managing Wealth

Introduction

From Norges Bank we can see the corner of the two streets, Tollbugaten and Kirkegaten.[*] This is where the Collett building was situated until 1939 when it was dismantled and moved to the Norwegian Museum of Cultural History at Bygdøy. By then, the Collett family

* I would like to thank Amund Holmsen, Marie Norum Lerbak, and Øystein Sjølie for their valuable assistance in preparing this lecture. I would also like to thank Helle Snellingen for her contribution to the translation of the Norwegian text into English.

had not occupied the building for years and their wealth was long gone.

Around the end of the eighteenth century, John Collett made a large fortune in the timber industry. He also ran the great Ullevål farm and by the time of his death in 1810 he was managing one of the country's largest wealth portfolios. Collett was also known to spend extravagant amounts on lavish parties. The Napoleonic Wars and the English blockade took a heavy toll on the family business. After his death, Collett's heirs insisted on maintaining an extravagant lifestyle as if the income was still intact. Their wealth rapidly withered away and in 1829 the coffers were empty. The farm was taken over by the state.[1]

The time it took Collett to make a fortune is about the same as it took Norway to build up its oil-based financial wealth. Nearly forty years after Phillips Petroleum discovered commercially viable oil reserves in the Ekofisk field,[2] we have an oil-based sovereign wealth fund worth more than NOK 3 trillion. Few other countries are sitting on such huge financial reserves. But our

---

[1] Alf Collet (1915), *Familien Collett og Christianialiv i gamle dage (The Collett family and life in Christiania in olden days)*, Kristiania: Cappelen.

[2] See *Facts 2011 – The Norwegian petroleum sector*, Ministry of Petroleum and Energy: www.npd.no/en/Publications/Facts/Facts-2011/.

wealth primarily comes from other sources than the oil fund, now called the Government Pension Fund Global. The value of our current and future labor resources is more than ten times as great as the value of our oil and the oil fund combined.[3] The oil fund would be depleted in three years if government tax revenues were to disappear entirely.

Our economic future depends above all on our capacity to produce goods and services that others value. But the visible oil revenues may give the impression that we have a huge treasure trove at our disposal. Sound wealth management is therefore first and foremost a question of maintaining and developing the value of our productive resources, particularly our labor resources.

A nation that comes into a large fortune must make a number of choices and trade-offs. They can be considered from a legal, ethical, or financial standpoint. In my speech today, I will discuss in particular what sound management entails from an economic viewpoint. I will also touch upon how we practice oil wealth management in Norges Bank.

[3] Report to the Storting on Long-Term Perspectives for the Norwegian Economy, Section 4.5: www.regjeringen.no/en/dep/fin/press-center/press-releases/2009/long-term-perspectives-for-the-norwegian.html?id=542381.

Intergenerational Saving

The first question that must be answered is: Who owns the oil wealth? Does it belong to the present generation of Norwegians? Does it also belong to future generations?[4]

Even though I will be speaking from an economic vantage point, I will borrow a point made by the philosopher Henrik Syse. He asks whether we have the *right* in the course of a single generation to expend resources that it has taken nature millions of years to produce.

But there are also counterarguments. The next generations are likely to be wealthier than us in any case. Should we save for them?

Saving for the future can also be supported with vicarious arguments by those who are worried about their own upcoming pension payments. Today's pension obligations are underfunded but can be more easily met if oil

---

[4] The intergenerational perspective was not mentioned in the first public document to contain a broad discussion of the role of oil in Norwegian society, Report No. 25 to the Storting of 1974. The focus was on how the government would spend the revenues from the oil sector to create a "qualitatively better society" – immediately. The oil deposits were not discussed as they are today as wealth to be invested. See Report No. 25 to the Storting (1973–1974): "Petroleumsvirksomhetens plass i det norske samfunn (The role of petroleum activity in Norwegian society)," Ministry of Finance.

revenues are saved. Is this the "1968 generation" that first went on a spending spree and is now arguing in favor of saving to secure their own pensions?[5]

Moreover, all we have to do is read today's press to understand that it is not a matter of course that economic growth will maintain its current pace. It is not a given that our children will be that wealthy.

For those with roots in agriculture, it is second nature to leave the farm in at least as good shape as when it was taken over. A policy of high and rising spending, which would crowd out internationally exposed industries and lead to unsustainable public expenditure levels, would be a heavy legacy to leave behind. The next generations would have to increase taxes substantially because of our consumption. If we, as a nation, set money aside instead, our wealth will grow and contribute to improving prosperity for our children.

Spending and saving are mutually exclusive actions. The definition of *saving* is quite simply to *abstain from*

---

[5] In 1985, Professor Steinar Strøm wrote that it was an understandable human reaction to celebrate Norway's new oil wealth with a spending spree. At the same time, Strøm pointed out that as oil revenues became substantial, money could be set aside in a fund abroad. Steinar Strøm (1985), "Oljemilliardene – Pengegalopp til sorg eller glede? (Norway's oil billions – curse or blessing?)," *Sosialøkonomen*, Vol. 1, p. 246.

spending. But with Norway's huge oil revenues and the return on the portion saved we can increase spending while accumulating considerable savings. But spending must be adapted to the return on the portion saved.

Sound and long-term management of oil wealth also requires separating saving decisions from spending decisions. The fiscal rule sets an important *cap.*[6] The rule states that petroleum revenues are to be saved, while the government may spend the return on the oil fund. Once the cap has been set, expenditures across worthy public programs must be made according to priorities – not by lifting the cap. If the ability to prioritize fails us and the cap is lifted, the long-term margin of maneuver will be reduced fairly quickly. Less will be left to our children.

As long as the North Sea generates revenues, the value of the fund will rise, laying the basis for a sustainable rise in petroleum revenue spending.[7]

---

[6] Report No. 29 to the Storting (2000–2001): "Guidelines for economic policy", Ministry of Finance.

[7] In 1977 the Canadian economist John Hartwick described the principles for the management of a natural resource in order to produce permanent income. See John M. Hartwick (1977), "Intergenerational Equity and the Investment of Rents from Exhaustible Resources," *American Economic Review*, Vol. 67, December, pp. 972–974.

Institutional Challenges

Oil converted into money entails institutional challenges. A crucial question that arose when we discovered oil was whether we had the discipline to refrain from spending all the money at once. In 1983, the Committee on the Future of Petroleum Activity was chaired by former central bank governor Hermod Skånland. He was of the view that it would not be possible to set aside a share of the oil revenues in a fund: "In the light of the prevailing attitudes among both politicians and the wider population, it is difficult to imagine that hundreds of billions will be invested in foreign assets while there are domestic needs that have not been met."[8] For Skånland the solution was simple. If the political system did not manage to set aside the revenues, the oil taps had to be opened very slowly. Wealth management could be carried out by portioning exploration sites in the North Sea. Oil that had not been discovered would burn a hole in the pockets of politicians to a lesser extent than money flowing into the state coffers.

Skånland's skepticism was well founded. Future oil revenues were used as an argument for allowing the central government to run a budget deficit. Moreover,

[8] NOU (Official Norwegian Report) 1983:27 "Petroleumsvirksomhetens framtid (The future of petroleum activity)," p. 90.

it would transpire that the actual pace of oil extraction – and oil revenue spending – increased much faster than the committee had recommended.

In the first twenty-five years, Skånland's prediction was right on the mark. All the oil revenues were spent. But in the past fifteen years, petroleum revenues have risen at such a fast pace that a portion has been set aside. If we look at the period of oil revenues in its entirety, close to half of the oil-based revenues have been spent.[9]

In 1994, the economists Bye, Cappelen, Eika, Gjelsvik, and Øystein Olsen of Statistics Norway estimated that government petroleum revenue spending came to about 10 percent of overall public expenditure at that time. Tax income from the petroleum sector and petroleum sales revenue – current petroleum revenues – were spent over the government budget. The economists at Statistics Norway expressed concern regarding Norway's oil dependence.[10]

---

[9] See Ministry of Finance calculations (Norwegian only): www.regjeringen.no/nb/dep/fin/tema/norsk_okonomi/bruk-av-olje penger-/hvor-mye-oljepenger-har-vi-brukt-sa-lang.html?id=450461.

[10] Torstein Bye, Ådne Cappelen, Torbjørn Eika, Eystein Gjelsvik, and Øystein Olsen (1994), "Noen konsekvenser av petroleumsvirksom-heten for norsk økonomi (Some of the consequences of petroleum activity for the Norwegian economy)," Statistics Norway *Rapporter* 94/1, p. 36 (Norwegian only).

These economists can now rest assured knowing that around 10 percent of public expenditure is still financed by oil money, but with one important difference from 1994: The source of these revenues is now the return earned on the oil fund – not current petroleum revenues. We have thus succeeded in replacing oil revenues with a permanent flow of income. We can draw on a perpetual source rather than from a well that is being depleted.

It may be that the oil fund has exceeded a critical value so that the ambition of a perpetual fund will be achieved. But history remains to be written. The story of John Collett might also have been written with a different pen when his wealth was at its peak.

Within a few years, as much as 15 to 20 percent of the welfare state could be financed by the return on the oil fund. But if we squander the capital in the fund, we will either have to match the shortfall with tax increases or make substantial cuts in government welfare. The gains – not only the costs – of building up an oil fund have thus been made visible. This also attracts its defenders.

Large fortunes nevertheless give rise to concerns. As a minimum requirement, the management of oil wealth must not impair the productivity of labor and real capital. This may seem to be a modest goal, but is not a trivial one.

People of my generation may remember the German Gunter Sachs, one of the heirs to the Opel fortune. He was known for saying that he had not worked a day in his life.[11] Sachs could live off his fortune and his spending was not confined to only useful things. For example, he lavished thousands of red roses on Brigitte Bardot, strewn over her home from a helicopter. There is no shortage of examples of individuals who have spent large portions of their wealth on an opulent lifestyle. But nations do not have the possibility of living off wealth alone. A nation thrives on each other's labor, as Finance Minister Erik Brofoss stated in his address on the state of the economy to the Storting in 1946.

The economists Jeffrey Sachs and Andrew Warner[12] have shown that countries with abundant natural resources have generally experienced weaker growth than otherwise comparable countries. Perhaps this is not so strange. Sudden wealth in one sector of the economy also results in higher wages and cost levels in other sectors. Such visible wealth can also weaken and crowd

---

[11] See, for example, the obituary "Gunter Sachs," *Telegraph*, 9 May 2011: www.telegraph.co.uk/news/obituaries/8503379/Gunter-Sachs.html.

[12] Jeffrey Sachs and Andrew Warner (1995), "Natural Resource Abundance and Economic Growth," NBER Working Paper 5398.

out internationally exposed business. Economists refer to this phenomenon as the "Dutch disease" after the Netherlands pursued an expansionary economic policy based on huge revenues from gas sales in the 1960s. When gas production declined, a period of harsh economic restructuring followed. The sheltered sector had to be reduced and the internationally exposed sector increased. There were too few left in the business sector to bear the welfare state.

The resource curse also increases rent-seeking at the expense of value creation, as the economist Trygve Haavelmo noted. Many countries that have experienced a windfall of wealth have been victims of this curse.

The state of Alaska has chosen its own institutional solution to avoid rent-seeking among special interest groups. Once the real value of Alaska's oil fund, the Alaska Permanent Fund, is secured, dividends are distributed to the owners. Each resident receives an annual cheque that can be spent as desired,[13] providing a strong incentive to protect the capital in the fund.[14]

---

[13] See, for example, the Alaska Permanent Fund website: www.apfc.org/home/Content/dividend/dividend.cfm.

[14] This would be comparable to using the return on the fund as tax relief.

The choice of building up a sovereign wealth fund must also be seen in connection with the state's substantial pension obligations under Norway's National Insurance Scheme. For the Norwegian state it would not have made sense to choose a solution like the Alaska fund without also addressing the issue of pension obligations.

So far our system has worked well, but the success of the system depends on broad-based support for government spending programs and the framework for saving oil revenues – the cap.

If the system fails and our wealth is spent on welfare schemes to the detriment of future labor income, our petroleum wealth may quickly become a bane. For example, if we were to slack off – intoxicated by the vast new oil fields Avaldsnes and Aldous Major in the North Sea – and reduce our work effort by extending our lunch break by five minutes every day, the sum of our future labor income will be reduced by as much as the value of our latest oil discovery.

Investments in Norway

How should oil revenues be saved?

An apt comparison is a family that wins a million kroner in the lottery. The family has to decide how to manage the newly found wealth.

- One option is of course to give it away or share the wealth.
- The family must then decide how much to spend and how much to save.
- The money can be spent on a long holiday or purchases for the home.
- If the family instead chooses to save the money, it will be faced with new choices.
  - Should the money be invested in a family-owned business?
  - In a neighbor's business?
  - Or should it be deposited in a bank or lent through another channel?

Even before discovering oil, the state had long been a substantial direct owner of Norwegian companies. The value of state investment in Norwegian companies is more than NOK 600 billion.[15] The state owns more

---

[15] Report no. 13 to the Storting (2010–2011) "Aktivt eierskap – norsk statlig eierskap i en global økonomi (Active ownership – Norwegian state ownership in a global economy)," Ministry of Trade and Industry (in Norwegian only), at www.regjeringen.no/pages/16193771/PDFS/STM201020110013000DDDPDFS.pdf, and the annual reports of the Government Pension Fund Norway and the Government Pension Fund Global.

shares in Norway than in the United States where the oil fund has its largest investments.[16]

But will substantial investment in one's own business – or one's own nation – guarantee growth and prosperity?

Many OPEC countries received enormous income after the oil price shocks in the 1970s. They later experienced not only low growth, but negative growth.[17] Professor Ragnar Torvik writes that one of the main reasons behind the decline was that such a large portion of the additional income was invested domestically. Politicians invested in projects that may have brought political gains – but resulted in economic loss.[18]

We can also draw on Norway's historical experience. In the postwar period, the Norwegian economy was to be reconstructed through a large-scale investment program.

---

[16] For fund holdings, see the NBIM website: www.nbim.no/en/Invest ments/holdings-/.

[17] National income in OPEC countries *decreased* on average by 1.3 percent annually in the period between 1965 and 1998 while OPEC oil production increased.

[18] See "Globalisering, olje og pensjonsfondet (Globalization, oil and the pension fund)," by Ragnar Torvik, available on the Ministry of Foreign Affairs website (Norwegian only) at www.regjeringen.no/nb/dep/ud/ kampanjer/refleks/innspill/oekonomi.html?id=491448.

Over several decades, the investment share of GDP[19] was close to 30 percent, markedly higher[20] than in other Western economies. But the Norwegian economy still expanded at a slower pace than those of nearby countries. A more efficient use of capital could have boosted consumption without negatively affecting economic growth.

The high investment level entailed human costs in that consumption of important goods were rationed. A visible cost was limited imports of fruit. As I recall, the selection of fruit and vegetables at that time would have made the recommended "5 a day" serving of fruit and vegetables far more difficult to follow than today.

In recent years, 15–20 percent of GDP has been invested in the mainland economy, or about the same percentage as our neighboring countries. But we are always faced with demands for more investment, which is perhaps not that surprising. All of us have probably been stuck in a traffic jam and felt irritation over poor road conditions. It is easy to agree that investment

---

[19] See national accounts data from Statistics Norway, www.ssb.no/hist stat/aarbok/ht-0901–355.html, and historical data on the Norges Bank website www.norges-bank.no/en/price-stability/historical-monetary-statistics/.

[20] See, for example, World Bank data on www.databank.worldbank.org.

in knowledge is sensible and of benefit for the future. But funding these investments by lifting the cap on petroleum revenue spending is a certain recipe for lean times. Many of us have perhaps driven along lightly trafficked roads of a strikingly high standard. Norway is already among the countries that invests most in education, without achieving particularly impressive results.[21] Norwegian companies that want to invest in profitable projects have access to a well-functioning capital market, both at home and abroad.

An absolute precondition for ensuring the sound management of our oil wealth is that investments in areas such as roads, education, cultural centers, hospitals, and sports centers are prioritized within the NOK 1 trillion allocated through the central government budget each year.[22]

In order to maximize the return on the substantial financial wealth owned by the government today, the oil fund must be invested abroad. But this gives rise to new trade-offs between risk, return, and ethical considerations.

---

[21] For the results of the Pisa survey, see www.pisa.no/english/index .html.
[22] www.statsbudsjettet.no/Statsbudsjettet-2012/English/.

Moderate Risk

First, let me look at the trade-off between risk and return. How should we invest our wealth without taking on excessive risk? When the oil fund is invested in other countries that are not as commodity-dependent as Norway, our overall national wealth will become more robust to oil price fluctuations.

Diversifying wealth does not of course insulate us from upturns and downturns. In autumn 2008, stock markets plummeted worldwide. There was nowhere to hide and the value of the fund fell by close to 25 percent. But the oil remaining under the North Sea lost even more of its value when oil prices fell from USD 150 to USD 40 in the course of a half year.

On the other hand, oil prices may show a more favorable tendency than equity prices. The slide in equity prices over the past quarter has not been accompanied by weaker oil prices.

Norges Bank has been delegated the responsibility for managing the Government Pension Fund Global and hence has an independent responsibility for limiting and managing risk. We have therefore reduced the fund's holdings of southern European government bonds. We have also reduced counterparty exposures to European banks.

Maximizing Returns

As a long-term investor, Norges Bank seeks not only to minimize the risk of losing wealth, but to maximize the return on the fund's capital within the risk limits set by the fund's owner. But how can we manage our wealth to promote capital growth?

Many have probably wondered, as does the poet Jan Erik Vold when he writes:

> You put
> as the advert says
> 20,000 kroner into a high-interest savings account
> in one of our largest banks. After six years
> you can go back to the bank and take out
> 35,532 kroner. The question is: From whom have they taken
> 15,532 Norwegian kroner?[23]

Vold has called this: "Capitalism's fundamental mystique – how a krone, by lying idle for a period of time, gives birth to a 10-øre coin." The poem is of course a few years old – both 10-øre coins and an interest rate of 10 percent (the rate in the poem) belong to the past.

---

[23] The poem "Kapitalismens grunnleggende mystikk (Capitalism's fundamental mystique)" is from Jan Erik Vold (1989), *Elg*, Gyldendal Norsk Forlag.

A krone that yields a return does not lie idle, however. It represents resources used to build production capacity. The 10 øre is value added generated when capital is put to work.

When our oil revenues are invested as financial assets abroad, we are buying a share of future global value added, which can subsequently be brought home and put to good use here.

As an investor, the oil fund in principle faces two alternatives: Should the fund be an owner by investing in equities, or provide loans to companies and governments by investing in bonds? The return in both cases essentially depends on developments in global trade and industry, on the world's economic future. Even our loans to governments depend on the success or failure of businesses since governments rely on tax revenues.

When we provide loans – by buying bonds – the borrower is obliged to pay us interest at fixed intervals and repay the principal at maturity. If the payment obligations are met by the borrower, the amount borrowed is recovered. In the event of a bankruptcy, bondholders are given higher priority than shareholders.

Holding shares therefore carries higher risk. Shareholders are last in line when a company's earnings are distributed. On the other hand, if the company thrives, potential gains are unlimited. This is why equity prices fluctuate relatively widely. We reduce the risk associated with equity exposures by spreading our ownership. We own equities in more than 8,000 companies.

To compensate for the higher risk, shareholders demand a higher expected rate of return. Over the past 110 years, returns have been on average 4 percentage points higher for shareholders than for bondholders every year.[24]

If returns on equities are higher than on bonds, perhaps as much of the fund as possible should be invested in equities.[25] Bond prices tend to fluctuate less than equity prices and tend to rise when equity prices fall. A good mix of equities and bonds can improve the relationship between risk and return.

The Ministry of Finance has assessed the trade-off between risk and return and decided, with the approval of the Storting, that 60 percent of the oil fund should be allocated to equities. The choice of equity allocation determines to a large extent the fund's return and risk,

---

[24] See Credit Suisse *Global Investment Returns Yearbook* 2011: https://infocus.credit-suisse.com/app/_customtags/download_tracker.cfm?dom=infocus.credit-suisse.com&doc=/data/_product_documents/_shop/300847/credit_suisse_global_investment_yearbook_2011.pdf&ts=20110326172226.

[25] Private investors, with shorter investment horizons, should have lower allocations to equities.

and is therefore one of the most important decisions concerning fund management. Almost 40 percent is invested in bonds, including government and corporate bonds, and a small portion is invested in real estate.[26]

Government bonds in particular were long regarded as safe investments. This was also the thinking behind Statens Reservefond (Government Reserve Fund), established in 1904 to provide for investment in "first-class" foreign securities, primarily French, German, and U.K. government bonds. High inflation in the wake of World War I reduced the real value of the fund by half, and the fund was discontinued in 1925.[27] Some would argue that investment in government bonds provides "risk-free returns." In the context of current developments in the euro area, it might be more accurate to refer to this form of investment as "return-free risk," to quote Yngve Slyngstad, the CEO of Norges Bank Investment Management (NBIM).

---

[26] For more about the Government Pension Fund Global's investment strategy, see the Norges Bank Investment Management (NBIM) website: www.nbim.no/en/Investments/.

[27] Aanund Hylland (2005), "Statens reservefond 1904–25. Et forsøk på å binde politisk handlefrihet? (The government reserve fund 1904–25. An attempt to bind the political room for maneuver?)," Norges Bank *Penger og Kreditt* No. 3, p. 182 (Norwegian only).

A third form of investment is the oil fund's direct purchases of real estate, so far in London and Paris. We buy large stakes – usually between 25 and 75 percent – in large real estate projects.[28] As a long-term investor, we hope to reap returns in this market as well.

A Large Investor with a Long-Term Perspective

When we buy interests in a company both ethical and economic considerations come into play. There are companies in which we do not invest. Companies that produce weapons in violation of fundamental humanitarian principles and companies that produce tobacco are excluded. Corruption or contributing to severe environmental damage may also lead to exclusion. About 50 companies are excluded.[29] There is often the dilemma of whether we should withdraw entirely from a company or enter into dialogue. If we withdraw, we lose a channel of influence.

We now own shares in more than 8,000 companies worldwide. As shareholders, we are entitled to vote when

---

[28] For more on the fund's real estate investments, see the NBIM website: www.nbim.no/en/Investments/asset-mix/Real-estate/.

[29] The Ministry of Finance decides which companies to exclude. For more on exclusion from the Government Pension Fund Global, see website: www.regjeringen.no/en/dep/fin/Selected-topics/the-government-pension-fund/responsible-investments/negative-screening-and-exclusion.html?id=447009.

important decisions are made about companies in which we have an ownership stake. Should we actively seek to influence developments or should we remain passive observers? Many large funds choose the latter. It requires time and effort to consider the issues to be addressed at a company's annual general meeting (AGM), and not least: We may be confronted with uncomfortable questions.

The fund now owns around 1 percent of the world's listed companies. This is both a lot and a little. For less than 0.1 percent of the global population to own 1 per cent of global equities is *a lot*. But 1 percent may seem *too little* to exert ownership influence.

Nonetheless, we have chosen to exercise our voting rights. In many companies, ownership is spread across many shareholders, in which case even a 1 percent interest is a large stake. The fund also has larger holdings – up to 10 percent – in a number of companies, which gives us the opportunity to steer companies in what we consider to be the right direction.

Voting is governed by a few main principles.[30] As a minority shareholder, equal treatment of shareholders and board accountability are two key elements of our long-term management.

---

[30] For more on ownership strategies, see the NBIM website: www.nbim.no/en/Investments/ownership-strategies/.

In addition, as the fund is invested in a wide range of companies with a long investment horizon, our concerns must go beyond the purely business-related. A manufacturing enterprise that emits pollutants and harms neighboring enterprises may not be of concern to the enterprise itself. But it is of concern to us because we own shares in the enterprises affected by the pollution. Water management and climate change are two of our strategic focus areas.

In addition to voting, we engage in dialogue with management teams in a number of companies. We must remember that when we point a finger at a company, we are also pointing a finger at the laws, regulations, and practices of the countries where the company legally operates. We make demands, yet we are at the same time a guest in our neighbor's house.

Excessive activism in other countries may defeat its own purpose. Skepticism toward foreign investors, and in particular toward large sovereign funds, is not an unfamiliar phenomenon. We could risk being perceived as a political fund rather than a financial investor. We have therefore chosen ethical guidelines and corporate governance principles that are based on OECD and UN principles.[31]

[31] For more about the UN guidelines, see "Global Compact": www.unglobalcompact.org/. For more on the OECD guidelines,

Our experience is that the fund is perceived as a welcome financial investor – not as a political player. Former South African central bank governor Tito Mboweni told me he preferred investments by the oil fund to development assistance. "Assistance means you feel sorry for us," he said to me, "investment means you believe in us."[32]

Conclusion

The larger the visible wealth is, the greater becomes the risk that sound management principles are relegated to the background. Both John Collett and Gunter Sachs had considerable wealth, and spent it generously all their lives. At the same time, both were interested in developing more permanent values through research. Sachs established an institute where advanced mathematical methods were applied to study the relationship between the position of the stars and the fates of human beings.[33]

see www.oecd.org/topic/0,3699,en_2649_37439_1_1_1_1_37439,00.html.

[32] South Africa received NOK 149.5 million in development assistance from Norway in 2010. See Norad website www.norad.no/en/tools-and-publications/norwegian-aid-statistics.

[33] See, for example, the obituary "Gunter Sachs," *Telegraph*, 9 May 2011: www.telegraph.co.uk/news/obituaries/8503379/Gunter-Sachs.html.

Collett was more down-to-earth. He studied new methods of crop cultivation and was a keen supporter of the cultivation of potatoes here in Southeastern Norway.[34] As a contributor to sustainable growth, we would have to say that Collett was closer to the mark than Sachs.

Norway's proximity to valuable natural resources has created substantial opportunities. New technology and new oil finds are still increasing the value of our oil wealth.

Two North Sea fields where oil and gas were recently discovered, Galtvort (Hogwarts) and Gygrid (Hagrid), have been given names from the Norwegian version of Harry Potter. One of the books features the lucky potion Felix Felicis. This magical potion is difficult to make. The consequences can be catastrophic if the ingredients are mixed incorrectly. But if mixed correctly, the drinker will succeed in all that he or she undertakes. The potion also has some highly detrimental side effects. If taken in excess, it may cause giddiness, recklessness, and dangerous overconfidence.[35]

---

[34] Sigurd Høst (1936), *Norges historie: med viktigere avsnitt av Danmarks og Sveriges historie. For middelskoler og ungdomsskole [History of Norway]*, Oslo: Gyldendal Norsk forlag (in Norwegian only).

[35] J. K. Rowling (2006), *Harry Potter and the Half-Blood Prince*, London: Bloomsbury.

On Managing Wealth

The economic policy choices made by the authorities and Norges Bank as manager of the Government Pension Fund Global must have legitimacy and credibility. Without long-term thinking, the management of our wealth will not be a success story. So far, it would seem that we have managed to mix and drink an adequate dose of Felix Felicis, but we must not let down our guard.

— ❖ CHAPTER FIVE ❖ —

On Learning from History: Truths and Eternal Truths

Introduction

All scientific and scholarly disciplines have a particular, and not immutable, set of truths.[*] Mathematics and theology are possible exceptions, though for different

---

[*] I have received valuable assistance in preparing this speech. Outside the Bank, I would like to thank Mike Bordo, Marc Flandreau, John Llewellyn, Henrik Mestad, Henrik Syse, and Knut Sydsæter. At the Bank, I would like to thank the following persons in particular for their contributions: Øyvind Eitrheim, Amund Holmsen, Jon Nicolaisen, Øystein Olsen, Øystein Sjølie, Birger Vikøren, and Mari Aasgaard Walle. I would also like to thank Helle Snellingen for her contribution to the English text.

reasons. As the late Professor Knut Sydsæter underscored when assisting me with this speech, in mathematics new results are proved on the basis of fundamental axioms and become new truths. Theology also relies on truths, even eternal truths. Even if logical proofs of God's existence have long been an important pursuit, it is safe to say that the truths in theology today stem from faith.

The discipline of economics can readily be formulated in the language of mathematics, and economic models are usually tested empirically before gaining acceptance. Conflicts arise when theories that appear to be patently true are unsupported by empirical evidence, or when contradictory theories find support at the same time. In other words, we economists are in a borderland between faith and the strict proofs of mathematics.

The notion of learning from history cannot easily be explored without invoking the American physicist Thomas Kuhn. This year is the fiftieth anniversary of the publication of his groundbreaking work, *The Structure of Scientific Revolutions*.[1] According to Kuhn, disciplines progress within an established set of truths – a paradigm.

---

[1] Thomas Kuhn (1962), *The Structure of Scientific Revolutions*, University of Chicago Press.

On Central Banking

Observations irreconcilable with the paradigm are tolerated as inexplicable. Eventually, however, the number of inexplicable observations can become so overwhelming that the paradigm breaks down. New truths have to be established – a paradigm shift occurs.

Such shifts can be painful. The old paradigm will usually be defended by those whose training lies in a more distant past, often persons in positions of leadership in academia and government bureaucracy.

Long before Kuhn, Henrik Ibsen touched upon the same idea in *An Enemy of the People*. Doctor Stockmann talks about the few who attain the new truths, unlike the compact majority that have yet to embrace them.

Social scientists, like economists, face some peculiar problems when attempting to learn from history. First, we do not have a laboratory in which we can perform experiments. Second, economic policy is part of the reality we observe. The outcome of a particular measure will depend both on shifting economic conditions and on economic agents' expectations of the effect of that measure. It goes without saying that in a situation like that, drawing useful lessons from history can be a challenge.[2]

---

[2] Here the natural sciences may be more stringent, and in some cases it may be easier to set up experiments that can refute the theory. For example, Einstein's theory of relativity was considerably

Scientific truths provide a common basis for further research and development, but they can be a scourge if they are not challenged. The recognition of economic correlations lays the groundwork for good economic

strengthened, and Newton's theory shown to be insufficient, during the solar eclipse of 1919. Scientists were then able to observe that the light from distant stars was bent by the Sun's gravity, just as Einstein had predicted. Many scientists once believed that the Earth looks the way it does, with mountains and valleys, because the Earth was originally a red-hot mass that gradually shriveled as it cooled. We know what an orange looks like after a long drying process or what clay looks like after being exposed to the air for a time. What was a smooth surface becomes wrinkled. In 1915 the German meteorologist Alfred Wegener proposed an alternative theory of *continental drift*. He used heuristic arguments based on studies of *coastlines*. Brazil has a coastline that is an apparent perfect fit with the Gulf of Guinea on the west coast of Africa. Even so, the theory was not accepted until it was given a proper theoretical foundation and empirical grounding. The breakthrough came fifty years ago, when the American geologist Harry Hess proposed his theory of *sea-floor spreading*, and by the end of the 1960s the theory of *plate tectonics* became established science. The Centre for Advanced Study, which is located here in the Academy, recently hosted a research group that is at the very international forefront of this field. Headed by Professor Trond Helge Torsvik, this group worked to incorporate the theory of plate tectonics into a broader theory of mantle dynamics as an explanatory model for movements in the Earth's crust. The aim is to understand the development of the Earth over several hundred million years. This is truly an ambitious example of learning from history. The Centre for Earth

policy, resulting in a better life for more people. The outcome can be disastrous if the established truths lay the foundation for bad economic policies. Economics as a discipline has in the past hundred years undergone several prominent paradigm shifts, with widespread impacts and implications.

What Have We Learned from 1930 to the Present Day?

More than five years have passed since the turbulence in financial markets began. Today's situation resembles the one former Norges Bank Governor Nicolai Rygg described in his annual address in 1933: "The figures for world output are truly disheartening. A recent estimate of the number of unemployed is an appalling 30 million." Except for the phrasing and style, that speech could be cut and pasted from that address in 1933 to describe the situation today. The queues of the unemployed that we used to see in 1930s vintage black-and-white photographs we are now seeing on television in living color. Youth unemployment in

Evolution and Dynamics at the University of Oslo was in November 2012 awarded the status of Centre of Excellence in research.

Southern Europe is especially high. The Red Cross is setting up food banks in Spain. The middle class is being hit by higher taxes, lower pensions, and unemployment. Political scientists tell us that this is a recipe for social and political unrest.[3]

In May 1945, the work began to rebuild our country after World War II. At that time, Friedrich Georg Nissen was the highest-ranking official in the Ministry of Finance. Nissen trained in the law, and the photograph of him in Einar Lie's book on the history of the Ministry of Finance shows a man formally dressed in a three-piece suit. He believed that the central government budget should be balanced each year. Fiscal policy was conducted based on this principle, which leading politicians also agreed with.[4] Tax revenue was to be spent, but not a penny more.

---

[3] Descriptions of the causes of the financial crisis that began in 1929 bear a striking resemblance to today's headlines: a massive and unregulated shadow banking system, global imbalances, and substantial income inequality (see John Kenneth Galbraith (1997), *The Great Crash, 1929*, Houghton Mifflin).

[4] "More than anyone else," Einar Lie writes, "he adhered to the fiscal policy convictions that he brought along to the postwar Ministry of Finance, which bore the stamp of his experience from a time without sufficiently stringent regulation of government finances." Einar Lie and Christian Venneslan (2010), *Over evne. Finansdepartementet*

Broadly speaking, the prevailing paradigm up until the Great Depression of the 1930s – both in economic policy and in economic theory – was that the authorities' role should be limited to keeping domestic order and ensuring a stable and predictable regulatory and operating framework. Prices adjust automatically to supply and demand, and the general view was that markets were self-correcting. Following the Depression, a new truth emerged, with John Maynard Keynes and Norway's own Ragnar Frisch at the forefront: prices and wages do not adjust that quickly – nor can we expect that markets will automatically ensure full employment. Hence, government should play a more active role in economic policy.

At the Ministry of Finance, Nissen kept to the traditional view. But the political leadership, and eventually the younger economists who started at the Ministry, had other plans.[5] The economy was to be managed. Keynes' idea that the budget should be used actively to manage demand and output was to them an obvious

1965–1992 [*Beyond our power. The Ministry of Finance 1965–1992*], Pax forlag.

[5] Einar Lie provides a detailed account of the break between classical and the new, more Keynesian thinking at the Ministry of Finance in the 2012 book *Norsk økonomisk politikk etter 1905* [*Norwegian economic policy after 1905*], Pax forlag.

truth. In a Kuhnian sense, the older civil servants had to go for the new thinking to gain ground. The legal experts at the Ministry had to give way to the young economists.

The new regulatory regime was enthusiastically implemented after the war, and crowned with success. The contrast between the blight of the interwar years and the postwar boom was stunning.

The ambition was not only to keep unemployment low. Which industry sectors should be allowed to invest? What type of dwellings should we build? Who should be able to buy a car and have a telephone installed? In the 1950s and 1960s, these were questions about which the central government had firm views.

Keynes's regulation and planning were predominant truths in the former government building for several decades. Yet these truths did not remain eternal. In the 1970s, deficits ballooned when the government used countercyclical policies to "build a bridge" over the global downturn. But it was a bridge to nowhere. Inflation took off and government finances were strained to breaking point. The policy of micromanaging the economy had gone too far. Wage and price controls at the end of the 1970s, the last gasp of the postwar paradigm, did little to help. Norway was close to being placed under IMF administration.

In fact, it was not possible to steer the economy toward permanent prosperity. The old doctrines collapsed.[6] New ideas for managing the economy took shape because the old system no longer functioned. Underlying the new truths was the notion that economic policy needed to operate through the proper market incentives and that economic policy must be sustainable and predictable. At the Ministry of Finance, the new ideas took hold primarily because a younger generation was taking over, just as when Nissen was pushed aside. Political micromanagement lost considerable traction.

Through the 1990s and up to the mid-2000s, economic growth was high and both inflation and unemployment low in much of the world. Cyclical fluctuations were moderate. The new truths appeared to be working well. This period is known as the Great Moderation. But underneath the positive developments, imbalances were building up both within and across countries.

As we have all experienced, it is easy to ignore the bill as long as the food keeps coming and the conversation keeps flowing. Countries and governments can live

[6] Hermod Skånland (2004), "Doktriner og økonomisk styring: et tilbakeblikk (Doctrines and economic management in retrospect)," Norges Bank's Occasional Papers No. 36, Oslo.

with deficits for a while, but sooner or later the bill has to be paid.

Budget deficits and high sovereign debt levels meant that the authorities had little slack when the financial crisis hit in autumn 2008.[7] Countries rapidly embarked on an unavoidable path of fiscal austerity at the very time that demand was falling and unemployment rising.

Unsound fiscal policies have particularly severe consequences when they coincide with a financial crisis. Capital markets were unable to manage the large pool of savings from emerging market economies in Asia. Safe yields had fallen and the search for returns provided fertile ground for creativity in financial markets. Governments worldwide allowed the banking system to grow in the belief that regulations were sufficiently stringent, that a large banking sector is a benefit, and that banks' self-interest would prevent them from taking excessive risk.

The regulations, which in the 1980s were regarded as overly rigid, had been introduced when the crisis of the

---

[7] Debt levels among European countries were, on the whole, excessive in 2008, though this varied substantially from country to country. For example, Ireland and Spain had moderate sovereign debt, but both countries later incurred additional obligations owing to the problems in their banking sectors. By 2008, the government debt of Italy and Greece had already exceeded 100 percent of GDP.

early 1930s was a still-vivid memory. The well-known Glass–Steagall Act had been passed in 1933 precisely to prevent financial sector excesses. Banks that took deposits from the public were subject to strict rules on risk-taking. Deposits were guaranteed by deposit insurance, and banks could draw on central bank liquidity if necessary. Investment banks whose customers were professional investors had a freer hand, but no safety net.[8]

---

[8] In the United States, under the Glass–Steagall Act, which was passed in 1933, banks were no longer allowed to engage in retail banking (deposits, lending, and payment services) while also engaging in more risky investment banking activities. When the act was formally repealed in 1999, it had long been the subject of intense discussion in the academic literature. See, for example, George Benston (1989), *The Separation of Commercial from Investment banking: The Glass-Steagall Act Revisited and Reconsidered*, Kluwer Academic Press; Randall S. Kroszner and Raghuram G. Rajan (1994), "Is the Glass-Steagall Act Justified? A Study of the U.S. Experience with Universal Banking before 1933," *American Economic Review*, Vol. 84, pp. 810–32; Eugene N. White (1986), "Before the Glass-Steagall Act: An Analysis of the Investment Banking Activities of National Banks," *Explorations in Economic History*, Vol. 23, pp. 33–55; and Charles W. Calomiris (2003), *U.S. Bank Deregulation in Historical Perspective*, Cambridge University Press. Marc Flandreau (2011), "New Deal Financial Acts and the Business of Foreign Debt Underwriting: Autopsy of a Regime Change," shows how the Glass-Steagall Act and other New Deal legislation conferred greater power on policy makers at the expense of international bankers and discusses some consequences for financial markets. Flandreau's article can be downloaded from Norges

Banking gradually became a growth industry in many countries. Strict regulations in one country prompted banks to flee to another. The result was the dilution or elimination of many regulations that attempted to rein in the imagination of the financial sector. The rationale behind the Glass-Steagall Act was discarded. This trend was universal. Unfettered financial markets were apparently a success. Mortgage-backed securities enabled more

Bank's website: www.norges-bank.no/Upload/82434/EN/FLAN DREU%20Paper.pdf.

In this area, there are few, if any, ultimate truths, and the pendulum appears to be swinging back again. In the United States, the United Kingdom, and the euro area, reintroducing some sort of separation between retail and investment banking is now being discussed; cf. the Volker Rule (United States), the Vickers Commission (United Kingdom), and the Liikanen Plan (European Union). Andrew Haldane at the Bank of England has recently discussed this issue in his speech "On being the right size," where he also outlines proposals for future banking sector regulation (see www.bankofengland.co.uk/publications/Pages/speeches/2012/615 .aspx). CEO Sandy Weill of Citigroup, the largest U.S. bank before the crisis, said in July 2012 that repealing this act had contributed more than any other factor to the financial crisis. See also the article "Roosevelt's Lessons for President Obama" by Marc Flandreau (2012), in the *Global Journal* (theglobaljournal.net/article/view/770/), where the author discusses historical perspectives on New Deal policies in the 1930s.

Americans to become homeowners, and a bullish stock market was good for pension funds – as long as it lasted.[9]

Big banks can easily give rise to big ideas about the importance of a country. But the financial crisis showed that big banks above all give rise to a political headache and a massive bill for taxpayers. Banks that are so large that they can undermine the entire financial system cannot easily be allowed to fail.[10]

---

[9] For decades, a number of policies have been implemented in a large number of countries, including Norway, to support home ownership. Raghuram G. Rajan (2010), *Fault Lines: How Hidden Fractures Still Threaten the World Economy*, Princeton, N.J.: Princeton University Press, describes U.S. housing market policies.

[10] Experience shows that governments routinely bail out banks on the verge of failing. Of course, this sort of implicit government guarantee makes lending to these banks safer, and reduces their borrowing costs. The difference between the rate they actually pay and what they would have had to pay without the implicit government guarantee amounts to a subsidy. Andrew Haldane at the Bank of England notes in his speech "On being the right size" that if we look at some of the world's largest banks, this subsidy amounted in the period between 2002 and 2007 to around half of posttax profits. When the financial crisis erupted, this implicit subsidy became explicit and was equal to more than posttax profits. By comparison, the value of the subsidy exceeds the amount spent globally each year on development assistance (see www.bankofengland.co.uk/publications/Pages/speeches/2012/615.aspx). However, this subsidy does not go to the needy. Figures for the United States show that CEOs of the largest investment banks earned 500 times the median U.S.

The Basel Committee on Banking Supervision seeks to ensure that different countries operate on a level playing field. While this is a good thing, the result was often compromise whereby the country with the weakest regulations set the standard. One must also recognize that the new rules introduced in the 1980s did not take into account banks' ability and creativity in terms of circumventing these rules. Rules intended to mitigate the risk of financial instability actually encouraged banks to take on ever more risk.

What do economists do when regulations do not work? Paradoxically, what we do is argue that we need to regulate more and better. There is now a third version of the Basel rules, which have grown from 37 to 616 pages.[11] Andy Haldane, Executive Director of Financial

household income in 2007, a ratio that has increased fivefold since 1989. Andrew Haldane discussed this recently in his speech "A leaf being turned" (see www.bankofengland.co.uk/publications/Pages/speeches/2012/616.aspx).

[11] Nevertheless, Basel II gives banks ample leeway to determine their own capital requirements. In 2007, the Swiss bank UBS held USD 50 billion in U.S. CDOs, but the bank believed that these were risk-free, since the paper had the highest rating from the rating agencies and the bank had also purchased credit default insurance. Thus, the bank did not have sufficient capital reserves to cover any losses on this portfolio (Gillian Tett (2009), *Fool's Gold*, New York: Free Press).

Stability at the Bank of England, estimates that, all together, the rules – once they are fully incorporated in national legislation in Europe – will number 30,000 pages.[12] Is this really the way to go? Has the pendulum swung too far?[13] Are we facing a new paradigm shift?

---

[12] Andrew Haldane (2012), "The dog and the frisbee," speech at the Federal Reserve Bank of Kansas City's 36th symposium "The Changing Policy Landscape," Jackson Hole, Wyoming.

[13] Swings of the pendulum are a frequently used metaphor in studies of financial crises. See, for example, Michael D. Bordo (2003), "Market Discipline and Financial Crisis Policy: a Historical Perspective," in George G. Kaufman (ed.), *Market Discipline in Banking: Theory and Evidence. Research in Financial Services: Private and Public Policy*, Vol. 15, Elsevier, pp. 157–182. According to Bordo, the pendulum swings between measures to prevent crises, manage crises, and resolve crises. Erik F. Gerding (2006), "The Next Epidemic: Bubbles and the Growth and Decay of Securities Regulation," *Connecticut Law Review*, Vol. 38, No. 3, pp. 393–453, shows how economic upswings are often periods of deregulation and overoptimism in securities markets, while the downturns that follow are marked by austerity and calls for stricter regulation. Moreover, regulations become less effective as time passes, and market participants forget the previous crisis. Gerding provides examples of such cyclical pendulum movements going as far back as the 1600s.

In Spite of Lessons Learned: Back to Square One

The philosopher Henrik Syse has reminded me of this very phenomenon. Truths we took to be eternal often prove to bear the stamp of their time. We then find new truths and throw out the old ones. Following the policy failures in the 1970s, many economists believed that Keynes and his disciples were wrong, and "Keynesian" almost became a term of abuse, referring to irresponsible government spending. But to draw such a conclusion is to go to extremes. Keynesian policy is often appropriate in a contractionary period, but it also involves saving in times of growth – a component that had been widely forgotten.[14]

---

[14] Georg F. Nissen was not alone in focusing on the fiscal balance. Nicolai Rygg wrote the following in 1948: "There is a tenet that is not difficult to endorse: in times of slow economic growth, when the private sector relaxes, central and local government should support the economy, initiate projects to sustain activity and to prevent a rise in unemployment. But the other side of this coin is also important: in years when economic conditions are favourable, when the private sector is at full speed, the government should hold back and put aside reserves to boost its financial strength so that it can provide support when the economy needs it." Nicolai Rygg (1948), "I økonomisk stormvær (In stormy economic weather)," festschrift for Joh. H. Andresen, also published as an annex to the periodical Statsøkonomisk tidsskrift nr. 3/4 1948,

On Central Banking

The economists Carmen Reinhart and Kenneth Rogoff have summarized the experience of financial crises all over the world over the past 800 years. They show that history repeats itself. The "truth" most often proclaimed in boom periods just before the bubble bursts is the belief that "this time is different," which is also the ironic title of the book.

Although history never repeats itself exactly, some key features recur: one recurring feature is that boom periods are confused with an increase in the economy's growth capacity. Good times are mistakenly interpreted as perfectly normal.[15]

When times are good, it is difficult to gain acceptance for setting aside funds. There are always unsolved tasks in a society, and these tasks attract attention. In the 1930s, Ragnar Frisch understood that it is difficult for politicians to recognize good times at the time. He

---

p. 23. In this article, Rygg highlights his assertion that government budgets must balance over the business cycle.

[15] Governments consistently overestimate growth in their forecasts (Jeffrey A. Frankel (2011), "Over-Optimism in Forecast by Official Budget Agencies and Its Implication," NBER Working Paper No. 17239). But this is difficult; in summer 2008, the average OECD country overestimated the budget situation in 2007 – the year prior to the forecast – in an amount equivalent to 2 percent of GDP (National Budget 2013).

believed that it was the task of economists to ascertain the cyclical situation.[16]

When the crisis arrived in 2007, government finances were in disorder. Deficits and debt rose to such high levels that it was difficult for many countries to borrow money. When credibility is lost and lenders draw the line, Keynesian policy has reached its limit. These countries now have no other choice than to cut welfare schemes and public spending. The political fury we are now witnessing in Athens, Madrid, and Rome is being directed at today's political leaders. Perhaps their rage should be directed at those who were in positions of responsibility in the good times, instead of at those who are now left with the washing-up.

We have furthered our understanding of economics over the many decades since Keynes, Frisch, and others laid the basis of modern economics after the 1930s crisis. Theories have become more advanced, and methods and calculations far more complex. We have reams of regulations.

Perhaps one lesson to be learned from history is that the simplest method can sometimes be the best, as Andy

---

[16] In his 1933 pamphlet "Saving and Circulation Regulation," Frisch proposed the establishment of an advisory committee on the business cycle, composed of economics experts.

Haldane has argued. Friedrich Georg Nissen's rule that budgets should always balance was not particularly sophisticated, but if his ideas had been followed before the crisis, many countries would now be better off.

However, the principles behind Nissen's ideas were not completely unfamiliar when European politicians drew up the Maastricht Treaty at the beginning of the 1990s. The treaty contained simple rules for economic policy: budget deficits should be below 3 percent and government debt below 60 percent of GDP.

The rules sparked debate, and academics the world over – including in Norway – ridiculed them as far-fetched and hopelessly rigid. And as so often before, the rules soon sank into oblivion, particularly after the major EU countries Germany and France had pushed them aside.

In retrospect, we can acknowledge that simple rules of thumb can often be useful. For my own part, many years' experience of economic policy has led me to notice the prevalence of the number 4.[17] A current account deficit exceeding 4 percent of GDP is often a harbinger of future problems. Spain is a case in point: government finances

---

[17] See Sigbjørn A. Berg, Jan F. Qvigstad, and Nikka H. Vonen (2011), "Two essays on the magic number 4," Staff Memo 2/2011, Norges Bank, and John Llewellyn and Jan F. Qvigstad (2012), "The 'Rule of Four,'" *The Business Economist*, Vol 43, No. 1.

were fairly healthy, but deficits were building up in the private sector. Inflation of more than 4 percent is usually a sign of economic instability. If unemployment in a country is persistently above 4 percent, there is probably something wrong both with the functioning of the labor market and with the level of political ambition. And the financial crisis has shown that total banking sector lending in the most heavily indebted countries has often been more than 4 times GDP.[18] In this situation, any rescue packages would be too expensive for taxpayers – Ireland and Iceland are two examples.

This is a familiar element in our everyday lives. Speed limits are an example of such a rule. Calculating the optimal speed for a specific car on a specific road is extremely complicated. It would require considerable knowledge of both mechanics and physics. Speed limits help us. Of course, it might be optimal to drive faster or slower than the speed limit, but the rule is simple to understand and easy to enforce. This simple rule helps

---

[18] The financial sector faces risk involving probabilities of various outcomes that we can forecast fairly accurately. But it also faces genuine uncertainty, where probabilities are also unknown. We do not know all the possible outcomes of bank behavior or the real probabilities. Such uncertainty is more effectively managed using simple and robust rules, rather than rules that are as complex as the systems they are meant to regulate.

to shape our behavioral patterns to ensure efficiency and safety in the traffic system.

Simple rules can also make it easier to resist the temptation to postpone problems. Economists call this the time inconsistency problem. Odysseus solved his time inconsistency problem by having himself tied to the mast and instructing his crew to plug their ears with wax and ignore him when he would later ask them to steer the ship toward the song of the sirens. That was an easy rule for the crew to follow.

But rules can be too simple.[19] They must be used only as points of reference, not as excuses for doing nothing. Economic policy rules should be common knowledge. An independent body should be established to tell us when we are "speeding," and procedures must be in place

---

[19] The psychologist and Economics Nobel laureate Daniel Kahneman touches on this theme in his book *Thinking, Fast and Slow* (Allen Lane, 2011) (see, e.g., page 98). Kahneman points out that the application of heuristics – simple decision-making rules often used to find answers to difficult questions – may produce answers that are imprecise or wrong. The use of heuristics may be regarded as a way of substituting complex questions with simple ones. While simple rules produce answers quickly, these answers may not be a proper response to the question we want to know the answer to. An analogy to this is substituting the fundamental question "Am I driving safely?" with "Am I obeying the speed limit?"

to implement measures to solve the problem.[20] The new "Fiscal Compact" in the euro area is a tightening of the Maastricht Treaty, precisely to prevent the simple rules from being broken.

[20] Most countries have balanced budgets as a long-term strategy. However, the long-term intention of a balanced budget is often abandoned in practice. This is another example of the time inconsistency problem. Today, many European countries are forced to pursue fiscal austerity, even if their current economic situation makes such a policy undesirable. The most rational option would be if governments were able to approve credible tightening measures that cut spending and raised taxes in the medium term, but that had negligible short-term austerity effects. Pension reform would be such a measure. The problem is that investors, who will be lending money to governments in the meantime, have little confidence that governments will actually follow through on their plans. History shows that they have good reason for this lack of confidence. Thus, the OECD and the IMF are recommending measures intended to deal with the time inconsistency problem and bolster confidence that long-term plans will actually be implemented. Independent fiscal policy boards that monitor government budgetary policy and that speak up if plans are not followed are one such measure. These boards will also make recommendations for realistic economic forecasting, so that projections of future tax revenues are credible. The idea is that greater credibility reduces borrowing costs and thus the need for cuts. The United Kingdom has basically followed up these recommendations by establishing the Office for Budget Responsibility (see www.hm-treasury.gov.uk/data_obr_index.htm). In the Eurosystem, there is now a tendency to give the Commission the role of

We should be less concerned about what is completely right and correct according to the prevailing truths, and more concerned about avoiding major mistakes, irrespective of what the truth might be.[21] And this is the line

monitoring member states' implementation of their own plans. Other countries, such as Denmark and Sweden, have fiscal policy boards, but in many cases they have taken on duties beyond those strictly related to remedying the time inconsistency problem. They also comment on how fiscal policy ought to be formulated. This quickly encroaches on what is properly the domain of politics, rather than helping the political system to be consistent in implementing its own plans. A more detailed discussion of fiscal policy boards, with a focus on the board in Sweden, is found in Egil Matsen, Gisle J. Natvik, and Ragnar Torvik (2010), "Finanspolitisk råd," Oslo: *Samfunnsøkonomen*, no. 2, pp. 11–19.

[21] The financial crisis has also reminded us of weaknesses in models and methods used in analyses behind the economic policies pursued. We must with humility acknowledge that we understand less about the functioning of the economy than we would have liked. Mervyn King, the Governor of the Bank of England, recently voiced this view in a speech, "Twenty years of inflation targeting," which he gave on 9 October 2012 at the London School of Economics (see www.bankofengland.co.uk/publications/Pages/speeches/2012/606.aspx).

Similar reflections have also recently been expressed in an interview with Andrew Haldane, the Executive Director for Financial Stability at the Bank of England, under the title "Our Models Are No Longer Working Properly" (see http://economicsintelligence.com/2012/10/24/bank-of-englands-haldane-on-the-crisis-of-economics-our-models-are-no-longer-working-properly/).

of thinking behind our inflation target for monetary policy and the fiscal rule for oil revenue spending.

We must be humble and constantly search for new knowledge. But as I have shown, there is a tendency for this humility to vary with the business cycle. Marc Flandreau and Mike Bordo tell me that during upturns, the colossal blunders of yesterday are forgotten by politicians, journalists, and central bank governors, but not by economic historians. And right now, their profession is enjoying its golden age.[22]

Simple economic rules can perhaps prevent countries from getting into difficulties, but once the rules have been broken and the crisis is a fact, the solution is anything but simple.

Real problems must be solved by real measures. That takes time and is painful, as we are witnessing in Europe today. Much of the adjustment in real terms is still to come, and there is still some way to

---

[22] In his article "Time on the Cross: How and Why Not to Choose between Economics and History," in Pat Hudson (2001), *Living Economic and Social History*, Glasgow: Economic History Society, pp. 81–85, Marc Flandreau gives a personal and colorful account of how he inadvertently and unwittingly and in the spirit of "having it both ways" became an economic historian, because he refused to choose between economics and history.

go before we will be able to say that the global economy is on safe ground.

The full consequences of inadequate regulation of financial institutions became visible only after the crisis was a fact. However, macroeconomic imbalances were widely recognized beforehand. In the mid-2000s, Federal Reserve Chairman Alan Greenspan raised the key rate to reduce the U.S. savings deficit. But long-term interest rates were kept low by the Asian savings surplus that found its haven in the United States. International organizations such as the IMF and the OECD pointed out what needed to be done, but the solution required measures to be implemented by a number of countries with differing interests and finding a good solution for the global community proved to be too difficult.[23]

The global community is nonetheless sometimes able to make decisions that benefit all countries. I witnessed this myself in Washington at the IMF's meeting in October 2008 following the Lehman Brothers collapse.

---

[23] Various observers have pointed out a number of factors that help to explain the financial crisis: Low key rates in all major countries over several years in the early 2000s, conflicts of interest in important financial institutions such as credit rating agencies, and considerable economic differences are just a few of them.

The alternative then was a black hole. In that kind of situation, it is easier to reach agreement.

In many ways, central banks are the response the authorities could apply when crises arose. Central banks were established to exercise control over the monetary system, enabling states to issue banknotes people could trust and providing banks with a bank for their own deposits and from which they could, in the last resort, borrow from in times of crisis.

Confidence in the monetary unit is the mainstay of our financial system. The following may serve as an illustration: It costs 50 øre to produce a banknote. For every 100-krone banknote Norges Bank issues, we apparently create wealth of NOK 99.50 – out of thin air. But people still sleep soundly in their beds – including those with money under their mattresses – because we are confident that the money can be exchanged for real goods.

It is, of course, tempting to take advantage of this confidence. History is full of kings and governments who have attempted to do just that. In 1716, the Scottish economist John Law established a bank that soon assumed the role as the first central bank of France. John Law saw the possibility of printing banknotes to finance promising development projects in the New World. Excessive confidence in the potential for profits fueled both the printing presses and equity prices in Paris. The bubble burst and John Law

fled to Italy.[24] Today, the European Central Bank and the
central banks in the United Kingdom and the United States
are using money they have produced themselves to

[24] Government debt in France had reached enormous proportions
after the Spanish War of Succession (1702–1713). After the death
of Louis XIV in 1715, John Law persuaded the French authorities to
convert government debt into equity capital in the Compagnie
d'Occident, also known as the Mississippi Company. The company
was awarded exclusive rights to develop the French territories in
North America and a number of trade privileges. Banque Générale
was taken over by the state, given the name Banque Royale, and
later merged with Mississippi Company. John Law was appointed
Contrôleur Général des Finances and now controlled in practice
France's finances and all trade between France and countries outside Europe. Banque Royale was given unlimited rights to issue
banknotes (*livres tournois*). This was the first time paper money had
been issued in France. The banknotes were made legal tender and
the bank was given the right to collect taxes. An increasing number
of stocks in the Mississippi Company were issued against government debt or paper notes issued by the Banque Royale. This led to a
speculative bubble and new rounds of share issues. The value of the
shares rose twentyfold in the course of 1719 and the number of
millionaires rose sharply. When some investors sought to sell their
shares in exchange for gold early in 1720s to secure their gains, the
party came to an end. The bank attempted to persuade investors to
accept banknotes instead, but this led to a sharp increase in the
money supply. Inflation surged and in January 1720 it had exceeded
20 percent per month. In late spring 1720, the bubble burst. People
lost all confidence in banknotes. Coins resumed their status as
means of payment, and to the extent that bank-like institutions

purchase government bonds and other securities. They are taking advantage of the confidence the central bank enjoys to buy time to enable European countries to tackle the underlying problems.

were established in France in the next 150 years banks were designated using other names such as "caisse," "credit," "société," or "comptoir." John Law was sacked and allegedly fled the country disguised as a woman. At about the same time a similar project in England led to the South Sea Bubble. Under an agreement between England and Spain in 1713, the South Sea Company was awarded a contract for delivering slaves to the Spanish territories in America. The South Sea Bubble also burst in 1720. In contrast to the Mississippi bubble, however, the South Sea Bubble involved extensive insider trading and fraud, and as a reaction new and stricter financial regulation was introduced in England through the Bubble Act and Sir John Barnard's Act. There is a large body of literature dealing with these speculative bubbles in France and England in the early years of paper money; see, for example, Larry Neal (1990, 2011), *The Rise of Financial Capitalism: International Capital Markets in the Age of Reason*, Cambridge University Press, and *I Am Not The Master of Events: The Speculations of John Law and Lord Londonderry in the Mississippi and South Sea Bubbles*, Yale University Press; Charles P. Kindleberger (1984), *A Financial History of Western Europe*, London: George Allen & Unwin; Gerding, "The Next Epidemic"; and John E. Sandrock (2007), "John Law's Banque Royale and the Mississippi Bubble," pp. 83–108, www.thecurrencycollector.com/pdfs/John_Laws_Ban que_Royale.pdf. For further details regarding South Sea Bubble, see Norges Bank's website, article by Helen Paul (2011), "Limiting the Witch Hunt: Recovering from the South Sea Bubble," www .norges-bank.no/Upload/82434/EN/PAUL%20Paper.pdf.

Some Lessons

Tonight's theme is "Learning from History." And in this title lies a question, in both the positive and normative senses. The answer to the question of whether we

Many decades were to pass before France reintroduced paper money. This was in connection with the French Revolution, which, paradoxically, also ended in disaster. The Revolution in 1789 led to substantial expenditures that needed to be financed. The Assemblée Nationale had reduced taxes, and instead issued large quantities of banknotes backed by confiscated church lands. These notes were called assignats, since each note was assigned to a specific property holding, which the bearer could subsequently take possession of. John Law originally had the same plan when in 1705 he proposed introducing land-backed paper money, but when Law was given the opportunity in 1715 to introduce paper money in France, the banknotes were collateralized by government debt and stock in the Mississippi Company. Meanwhile, French assignats were issued in such great quantities that the result in a few short years was hyperinflation that culminated in 1795. It would take years to restore confidence in paper money and banks in France. Sweden had a similar experience with paper money following an economic collapse in the 1750s. For that reason, Sveriges Riksbank was not permitted to print banknotes when it was founded. In Norway, Jørgen Thormøhlen (also known as Jørgen Thor Møhlen) issued banknotes in September 1695. His venture lasted a year! See Anders Bjarne Fossen (1978), *Jørgen Thormøhlen. Forretningsmann, storreder, finansgeni [Jørgen Thormøhlen. Businessman, shipping magnate, financial genius]*, Bergen: Einar Blaauw AS.

actually learn from history would probably have to be "yes and no." Sometimes we learn, sometimes we do not. Economic crises seem to be a necessary precondition for learning. And this may still be the case. We have some capacity to learn from our own mistakes – particularly if they are traumatic enough – but limited capacity to learn from other people's mistakes. This is something we recognize from raising children. To the frustration of their parents, children seem to be more interested in having their own experiences than listening to parents' advice, however good it might be.

The answer to the normative question "should we learn from history?" is obviously "yes."

And Which Lessons Should We Learn?

Allow me to venture to select three lessons on the basis of what I have said so far. First: *the simplest solution is often the best*. Simple rules, whether for fiscal policy or banking regulation, will often prevent the worst errors. And when the yellow warning light starts flashing, action must be taken. Second: *confidence is essential*, also for economic policy. Confidence is easily eroded and difficult – and costly – to restore. Confidence must be earned. The resolution of today's crisis will also follow a smoother path if there is confidence in institutions – banks, central banks, and governments. Borrowing costs will then decrease more quickly, the need for government spending cuts will diminish accordingly, and the good times will return sooner. Third: *we have no magic wand.* If a country has real economic problems, real adjustments must be made to solve them.[25] Central banks cannot solve the problems, but what they can do is lend money when there is none available elsewhere, giving countries more time to implement necessary reforms. Deficits must be reduced.

Unrestrained printing of money has led to problems on many occasions through history. If printing money is not followed up by action – in euro area countries, in the United Kingdom, and in the United States – Mario Draghi, Mervyn King, and Ben Bernanke run the risk of being recorded in history in the same chapter as the Scotsman John Law.

---

[25] In Act I of Part II of Goethe's *Faust*, published in 1832, the Emperor is in financial difficulties. Mephistopheles convinces him to print paper money backed by gold that has yet to be mined to boost economic activity. This works for a while, until soaring inflation destroys the economy. Jens Weidmann, the President of the Bundesbank, spoke of the dangers posed by overly unrestricted monetary policy, based on *Faust*, during the festival "Goethe und das Geld" in Frankfurt in September 2012: www.bundesbank.de/Redaktion/EN/Reden/2012/2012_09_20_weidmann_money_creaktion_and_responsibility.html.

On Learning from History: Truths and Eternal Truths

The full title of my speech today is "Learning from History: Truths and Eternal Truths." I have ventured to outline three lessons that are hopefully universally valid. But we can never be sure. I mentioned Ibsen's *Enemy of the People*. Allow me to conclude with Doctor Stockmann's comments: "Yes, believe me or not, as you like; but truths are by no means as long-lived as Methuselah – as some folk imagine. A normally constituted truth lives, let us say, as a rule seventeen or eighteen, or at most twenty years – seldom longer."[26]

Ibsen's play has been stood the test of time. It is still performed all over the world, 130 years after it was written. Not because the Norway of the 1880s never loses its appeal, nor because Doctor Stockmann found eternal truths. It is because the play raises questions of a more enduring nature. Perhaps we have to recognise that the closest we can get to eternal truths is, precisely, eternal questions?

---

[26] The quotation continues: "But truths as aged as that are always worn frightfully thin, and nevertheless it is only then that the majority recognises them and recommends them to the community as wholesome moral nourishment. There is no great nutritive value in that sort of fare, I can assure you; and, as a doctor, I ought to know." These "majority truths" are like last year's cured meat – like rancid, tainted ham; and they are the origin of the moral scurvy that is rampant in our communities.

— ✤ CHAPTER SIX ✤ —

On Institutions: Fundamentals of Confidence and Trust

Institutions

The concept *institution* has many meanings.[*] For example, there is an important distinction between its meaning as an abstract concept and as a concrete one. The *judicial system* in Norway is an institution in an abstract sense, while the *Supreme Court* is concrete. The *Norwegian National Opera and*

[*] I have received valuable assistance in drawing up this speech, in particular from Mike Bordo, Arne Jon Isachsen, John Llewllyn and Anders Vredin outside Norges Bank, and from Norges Bank staff; Øyvind Eitrheim, Amund Holmsen, Marie Norum Lerbak, Inka Rogne, Øystein Sjølie, Birger Vikøren and Lars Fredrik Øksendal. I would also like to thank Hellen Snelligan for the translation into English.

On Institutions: Fundamentals of Confidence and Trust

Ballet is a concrete cultural institution within our more abstract *cultural heritage*. In my own field, the *monetary system* is abstract whereas *Norges Bank* is concrete.

I would like to speak about the role institutions can play in the economic advancement of a nation and use the central bank as an example.[1] My co-speakers will view the issue from different perspectives and the ensuing debate will bring forth yet further aspects.[2]

---

[1] Among the many who have shed light on the role of institutions from this perspective is Douglass C. North, a 1993 Nobel Laureate in Economics together with Robert W. Vogel. In his work, he refers to institutions as follows: "Institutions are the rules of the game of a society and in consequence provide the framework of incentives that shape economic, political, and social organization. Institutions are composed of formal rules (laws, constitutions, rules), informal constraints (conventions, codes of conduct, norms of behaviour), and the effectiveness of their enforcement. Enforcement is carried out by third parties (law enforcement, social ostracism), by second parties (retaliation), or by the first party (self-imposed codes of conduct). Institutions affect economic performance by determining, together with technology employed, the transaction and transformation (production) costs that make up the total costs of production." See Douglass North (1997), "Prologue," in John K. Drobak and John V.C. Nye (eds.), *The Frontiers of the New Institutional Economics*, San Diego: Academic Press, p. 6.

[2] Economists use a basic and powerful theoretical construct to demonstrate that, at the most fundamental level, production takes place through the use of labor, capital, and raw materials as well as through technological progress. Lying behind it – and often having a profound effect on it – is how firms and the society in which the firms operate are organized. And organization is about institutions

On Central Banking

Good institutions provide sound frameworks that increase confidence and promote economic progress. This is so in relation to minor, everyday situations as well as to major life choices. At the fishmonger's, the *Norwegian Metrology Service* ensures that you pay for the actual weight of your cod fillet. When you buy a home, clarity about ownership and encumbrances is ensured by the *land register*.[3] The *Norwegian Industrial Property Office* grants patents so that entrepreneurs can make profits on their innovations. In the absence of such institutions, each of us would have had to spend more time on taking precautions and fewer investments would have been profitable.[4]

in the broad sense – everything from society's moral norms to how production is organized in each firm.

[3] Hernando de Soto in *The Mystery of Capital* (2000; New York: Basic Books) argues that a lack of proper land registration in poor countries makes it impossible for the poor to obtain credit. As a result, a large proportion of the population is in effect barred from establishing a business.

[4] The Arab sociologist and diplomat Ibn Khaldûn analyzed the relationship between institutions and economic progress. He published his major work in 1377. The book was published in Norwegian in 2013 under the title *Al-Muqaddimah. Introduksjon til verdenshistorien* (*Introduction to World History*), translated by Abdel Magid Al-Arakion. In 1759, in his work Theory of Moral Sentiments, Adam Smith wrote that institutions are the framework for progress. Good institutions promote confidence and thereby efficiency in society. The Norwegian American Thorstein Veblen, 115 years ago, described institutions as

However, in and of themselves, institutions are insufficient to ensure progress – the key is whether they are strong or weak.[5] This is also the starting point for Daron Acemoglu and James Robinson's book *Why Nations Fail.*[6] They introduced the concepts of *inclusive* and *extractive* institutions.[7]

the building blocks of economic development (see *The Theory of the Leisure Class: An Economic Study of Institutions*). In newer Norwegian research, Halvor Mehlum, Kalle Moene, and Ragnar Torvik have documented that institutions determine whether a country will manage to utilize discovered resources (see "Institutions and the Resource Curse," *Economic Journal*, Vol. 116, pp. 1–20).

[5] The young and already internationally renowned economist Jeffrey Sachs called on the then-Secretary General of the OECD, Jean-Claude Paye, immediately after the collapse of the former Soviet Union. Sachs claimed that all that was needed to get the economy moving was to liberate Russia's animal spirits. Paye demurred, saying that he thought that institutions would matter too. Sachs countered, saying, "But you are French, and so you think that institutions are more important than they really are." To which Paye replied, "And you are young, and take your institutions too much for granted." And then he added, almost as an afterthought, "If you do not have good, strong institutions, all you will get will be the mafia." E-mail correspondence from John Llewellyn, former colleague of Paye, dated 3 November 2013.

[6] D. Acemoglu and J. Robinson (2012), *Why Nations Fail: The Origins of Power, Prosperity and Poverty*, New York: Crown Publishers.

[7] Acemoglu and Robinson are not alone in attempting to capture institutional differences using concept pairs. In a historically based

- Inclusive institutions do not forget why they exist: they remember that their purpose is to serve the people, as the term "public servant" aptly illustrates. A well-functioning constitutional state makes cooperation and transactions simpler and cheaper.
- Extractive institutions, on the other hand, are found in countries where rulers govern without notable

social analysis, North, Weingast, and Wallis use the distinction between *natural state* and *open access societies* as reference for stage of development. The former was a strongly hierarchical society with tightly woven personal bonds with a clear social order. Collaborating elites had a monopoly on violence and dictated the allocation of resources. In an open- access society, on the other hand, the state holds power but there are institutional constraints. Political leadership has support from relatively broad economic and social groups, with more impersonal relationships and hence stronger competition and mobility. The authors argue that the transition between development stages to what they refer to as "the second social revolution," a somewhat broader concept than the Industrial Revolution that gives weight to, inter alia, the Enlightenment and modernity, started over 200 years ago, and that it is still underway. In many countries, society has benefited from technological progress but is still captive of the old stage of development of personal power relationships. They point to a clear concurrence between the open-access society and economic prosperity. Douglass C. North, John Joseph Wallis, and Barry R. Weingast (2009), *Violence and Social Orders: A Conceptual Framework for Interpreting Recorded Human History*, Cambridge University Press.

opposition, where the judicial system is not fair, and where rights are not equal for all.

The authors refer to several examples where people groups with identical backgrounds and access to the same natural resources have developed differently because of institutional differences.[8]

---

[8] Nation-building is a difficult task if there is no trust in as vital an institution as the police.

Professor of law at the University of Oslo Johs Andenæs spent the spring semester of 1971 as a visiting fellow at Oxford, taking along his son Ulf, who was my schoolmate. That year, Leszek Kołakowski, one of the past century's most famous philosophers, was also a visiting fellow at Oxford, and Johs Andenæs and Kołakowski became friends.Although Kołakowski had been one of Marxism's prominent postwar thinkers, by 1971 he had completely lost faith in the ideals of his youth. His relationship with the same communist authorities that he had served as an ideologist earlier in his life was becoming increasingly difficult. When the end of Kołakowski's visiting appointment neared, Johs Andenæs was told privately that Kołakowski was debating whether to defect and remain at Oxford. Kołakowski was particularly repelled by a fellow Pole who was also a guest professor and whose loyalty to the regime he believed was sheer opportunism. To Johs Andenæs, Kołakowski spoke of his countryman thus: "He is a criminal. He cooperates with the police!" As a professor of criminal law, Johs Andenæs found this to be an interesting statement. Kołakowski, for his part, did not return to Poland when his visiting fellowship ended soon afterward, but defected and became a leading critic of Marxist theory and practice

This leads to a key question: what are the principles that underlie those institutions that actually fulfill their role and effectively serve society?

A relevant starting point – as we are now approaching the bicentenary of the Norwegian Constitution – is 1814. This was the time when key nation-building institutions were founded, such as the Storting (Norwegian parliament), the Supreme Court, the University of Oslo, and Norges Bank. By the mid-1800s, civil society was also developing rapidly, as illustrated by the surge in the number of associations. The historian Jan Eivind Myhre has described this development in his book on Norway's history from 1814 to 1905. He relates, for example, that sixty clubs and associations were established in Løten in Hedmark county between 1850 and 1898.[9] These ranged from shooting clubs, cycling clubs, choirs, and agricultural associations to local political, missionary, and workers' associations. An array of common arenas boosts trust between people in a society. Trust in strangers helps oil the machinery. If you are able to trust the other party

---

and one of the intellectual fathers of Solidarity and the fall of communism.

[9] Jan Eivind Myhre (2012), *Norsk historie 1814–1905: Å byggje ein stat og skape ein nasjon* [*Norwegian history 1814–1905: Building a state and creating a nation*], Oslo: Det Norske Samlaget.

to the contract, you do not have to hedge against all possible outcomes.[10] The wheels of business turn faster and more smoothly.

The 1800s were characterized by upheaval and a change in the pace of economic development. In *the old society*, safety lay in close-knit networks and small institutions: the family, relatives, and neighbors. Once the pace of development picked up, however, these networks and institutions were no longer sufficient. New ones were needed.

Local savings banks are a good example. Specialization, market focus, and new tools demanded more financial muscle than the old, family-based networks could mobilize. The solution was for villages to join forces to create

---

[10] The level of trust in a society is influenced by many conditions. It may be that the recent years' large migration flows are eroding the trust that has prevailed in Norway earlier. However, immigrants have in fact adopted surprisingly rapidly the level of confidence in their new home country. See also Dag Wollebæk (2013), "Truer innvandringen tilliten? (Does immigration undermine trust?)," *Aftenposten*, 13 January, pp. 4–5. Alexander Cappelen and Bertil Tungodden at the Norwegian School of Economics are also working on these issues (see, e.g., http://paraplyen.nhh.no/para plyen/arkiv/2012/juni/tillitstesten/). See also Algan and Cahuc (2010), "Inherited Trust and Growth," *American Economic Review*, Vol. 100, No. 5, pp. 2060–2092, which documents a strong causal relationship between trust and economic prosperity.

savings banks, an institution rooted in the local community but reaching beyond the old networks. Løten Savings Bank opened in 1855.

A good public school system is a prime example of an inclusive institution. In May this year, I had the pleasure of visiting Stavanger Cathedral School. The head teacher, Turid Myhra, showed a portrait of one of her predecessors, Johannes Steen; schoolmaster, statesman, and nation-builder.[11]

Steen was notably a key driving force behind what was to become an important milestone in the construction of

---

[11] Johannes Steen (1827–1906) was born in Christiania (now Oslo). After completing a higher degree in philology at the University of Christiania in 1848, Steen held a number of positions in the school system and was for many years the headmaster of the Stavanger Latin School. Steen was also a member of the Storting and prime minister. Both as an educationist and as a politician, Steen made key contributions to the creation of the Norwegian comprehensive school. (Source: *Store Norske Leksikon*, http://nbl.snl.no/Johannes_Steen/utdypning.)

Internationally, the Society of Jesus is known as the founder of the modern school system, with a curriculum tailored to the child's age and previous knowledge and schooling characterized by systematic progression. These pedagogical principles evolved gradually through the second half of the 1500s, culminating in 1598 with *Ratio Studiorum*, the official plan for Jesuit education (see J. W. O'Malley (1993), *The First Jesuits*, Cambridge, Mass.: Harvard University Press).

Norway's collective identity: the adoption of the Primary School Act in 1889. The result was a comprehensive school system that strengthened our collective identity.[12]

For Norwegians, it is easy to take inclusive institutions for granted. Throughout human history, however, it is extractive institutions that have been the norm. There were attempts to achieve a balance of power in regimes as disparate as ancient Rome, China, and Venice. But they remained attempts. The inclusive institutions were replaced by nepotism and abuse of power.

The economists Acemoglu and Robinson point to the Glorious Revolution in 1688 as a turning point in history.[13] The British Parliament permanently curtailed the power of the Crown. The United Kingdom did not become a democracy in the modern sense overnight, but checks and balances were introduced. The development of written laws and a judicial system featuring

---

[12] Compulsory military service is also often quoted as a common area in which people from different backgrounds met on an equal footing, and often formed closer bonds. Accordingly, the Norwegian Armed Forces have not only helped to protect the country, but also developed Norway's social capital, at least that of half the population (see also N. R. Langeland (2013), "Møtet med krigens ånd (Meeting the spirit of warfare)," *Morgenbladet*, 1 November).

[13] D. Acemoglu and J. Robinson (2012), *Why Nations Fail: The Origins of Power, Prosperity and Poverty*, New York: Crown Publishers.

independent courts started. Patent laws were adopted and limited companies saw the light of day. The Bank of England, which was established in 1694, was controlled by the Crown's creditors. This limited the Crown's scope for printing money freely. Acemoglu and Robinson maintain that the Glorious Revolution paved the way for the Industrial Revolution.[14]

The Monetary System

A man who makes pins on his own can make between one and twenty pins a day. However, if the work is distributed among several workers such that one produces the wire, another straightens it, someone else cuts it to size, yet another sharpens it, and so on, ten men can produce 48,000 pins per day.

This is Adam Smith's famous example, taken from *The Wealth of Nations*, of how the division of labor is important for productivity and economic prosperity.[15]

---

[14] Not everyone agrees on this view of the *Glorious Revolution*. See, for example, N. Sussman and Y. Yafeh (2004), "Constitutions and Commitments: Evidence on the Relation between Institutions and the Cost of Capital," CEPR Discussion Paper 4404.

[15] Adam Smith (1776), *An Inquiry into the Nature and Causes of the Wealth of Nations*, Strahan and Cadell, reprinted 1937, New York: Random House

In Smith's example, all the operations take place within a single factory. But in a more complex society, one firm's output is another firm's input. An important prerequisite for such division of labor is that there are institutions that facilitate simple trading of what is produced.

The monetary system is an institution that simplifies trade in goods and thereby promotes the division of labor, productivity, and economic prosperity. We must bear in mind that money and the monetary system are not a goal per se. Money is like oil in the machinery.

Nevertheless, of all the systems existing within a state, the monetary system is among the more mystical when examined closely.

Historically, the king issued money, initially in the form of coins. His stamp turned the coins into a means of payment, and his power underpinned the monopoly on the issue of coins. Many kings managed their coinage. One example is Henry VII, the father of the modern English coinage system, whom historians have identified as an early proponent of healthy money.[16] His son, Henry VIII, was not as successful. From school, we best remember him for his high turnover of wives. To coin collectors, on the other hand, he is associated with the Great

---

[16] David Sinclair (2001), *The Pound: A Biography. The Story of the Currency That Ruled the World*, London: Arrow Books, pp. 141–142.

Debasement, whereby the silver content of one coin after another was diluted.[17] Neither the turnover among his wives nor the debasement of the coinage was conducive to building confidence.

The king could solve a short-term financing problem by issuing debased coins and more notes. However, with ever more coins and notes chasing the same goods, the long-term consequence was rising prices. Economists refer to this as an *inflation tax*.[18]

What happens when executive powers unleash inflation?

- First, confidence in money as a *store of value* disappears. An extreme example is the 1923 hyperinflation in Germany, when absolutely everything, including perishable food products, provided better security than money.[19]

---

[17] Between 1526 and 1542 the silver content of the circulation coin *groat* was reduced by 23.2 percent while the coin retained its nominal value of four pence. The king's gross seignorage increased from 2.1 to 20.1 percent. Debra Glassman and Angela Redish (1988), "Currency Depreciation in Early Modern England and France," *Explorations in Economic History*, Vol. 25, No. 1, pp. 75–97.

[18] Normally, it is Parliament's responsibility to appropriate money and the Crown's prerogative to spend it. When taxation occurs through inflation, this rule is broken.

[19] One of the classic accounts of hyperinflation is provided by Adam Fergusson (1975), *When Money Dies: The nightmare of the Weimar Hyper-Inflation*, London: William Kimber & Co.

- Second, money disappears as an *accounting unit*. Goods became the new standard. During the Napoleonic Wars, inflation was also very high in Norway, and the local history of the islands of Karlsøy and Helgøy shows that accounts were kept in silver or goods such as cod liver oil, pollock, and flour rather than speciedalers.
- Finally, money ceases to function as a *means of exchange*. After World War II, German industrial workers were paid in the firm's own products. Cigarettes and nylons functioned as a general means of payment.[20]

I mentioned that the monetary system seems to be shrouded in a veil of mystique. Initially it was not so. A coin's value was equal to its weight in silver. In our

---

[20] Owing to a lack of reliable means of payment, the recovery of production capacity and commerce in Germany after the war came to a standstill. On Sunday, 20 June 1948, under the direction of Ludwig Erhard, a large-scale currency reform was carried out in the western zones of occupation. The introduction of the Deutsche Mark was followed by measures to deregulate the economy and dismantle price controls. Virtually overnight, goods were available in the shops again. In the wake of these reforms, the Bank deutscher Länder, the precursor of the Bundesbank, was founded. The launch of the Deutsche Mark was an institutional prerequisite for the beginning of the postwar German Wirtschaftswunder. The successful reform bolstered the reputation of the monetary policy authorities and provided fertile soil for the trust the Bundesbank has enjoyed as a defender of stable money up to the present day.

day, the promise of precious metal has been replaced by the central bank's promise of price stability. Underpinning this promise is an institution, that is to say a bureau of statistics, that can measure general price developments, normally by means of a consumer price index. The statistics bureau must be independent of the political authorities, unlike in Argentina recently where the director was replaced because the government did not like the price figures.[21] Or unlike the situation in Norway in

---

[21] The events in Argentina in 2007 led to the initiation of a research project at the MIT Sloan School of Management to collect price data from retailers on a daily basis using scraping technology. The project, currently referred to as the Billion Prices Project (see http:// bpp.mit.edu/) is primarily associated with the MIT researchers Alberto Cavallo and Roberto Rigobon. The project started on a very small scale in 2007 when Cavallo used the technology to collect price data from supermarkets across Argentina, and he showed that inflation in Argentina was between twice and three times as high as reported in the official figures.

Today, the project is being continued under the direction of the private company PriceStats, which provides data collection and processing services. The Billion Prices Project currently involves the collection of price information from more than seventy countries and daily inflation series are published for over twenty of them. Fortunately, Argentina proved to be the only country where price indices using the new scraping technology were systematically on a much higher level than the official inflation figures. Thus, it appears that in today's open societies, it is difficult to conceal true

the 1950s, when the government subsidized some goods in the index to avoid automatic wage increases.[22]

developments. Incidentally, Argentine inflation figures from Price-Stats continue to show much higher inflation than the official figures (see www.pricestats.com/argentina-series). From February 2012, the *Economist* has replaced the official inflation figures for Argentina in its statistical tables with inflation figures compiled by PriceStats.

[22] Index manipulation is a demanding enterprise that often resulted in perverse economic incentives, sometimes with entertaining results. After 1945, a stabilization strategy was one of the cornerstones of the government's economic policy, and prices were to be kept stable as a way of navigating through the economic cycle. In July 1948, the Ministry of Trade received an offer to purchase a consignment of part-skim Danish Gouda cheese, a food item that was included in the cost-of-living index. Despite the bargain offer, the import price would have been higher than the selling price, so that subsidies would be necessary to avoid impacting the index. The end of the story was that a consignment of full-fat Gouda was imported, an item that was far more expensive, but that was not included in the index. Einar Lie (1995), *Ambisjon og Tradisjon. Finansdepartementet 1945–1965 (Ambition and Tradition. The Ministry of Finance 1945–1965)*, Oslo: Universitetsforlaget, p. 121.

A few years ago, the news website TV 2 Nettavisen revealed that the large grocery chains adjusted the prices of goods they knew were included in price tests conducted by the media in order to come out favorably in the tests. For example, the price of hand soap in a pump dispenser is lower than the equivalent quantity in a refill package (www.nettavisen.no/okonomi/privat/article373382.ece).

The monetary system has also become more intricate along another dimension. Today, cash accounts for only 5 percent of the money supply. Payments are primarily made using deposit money, which involves electronic signals created by the banks themselves, via cards, mobile phones, or online payments.[23] Millions of transactions between individuals, companies, and banks take place every day. These payments are settled at Norges Bank four times daily by transferring money between banks' accounts in Norges Bank. Norges Bank does not regulate the issuance of deposit money directly. By setting the interest rate on banks' sight deposits with Norges Bank and by securing settlements between the banks, the

---

[23] According to the economist Stephen Quinn, secure central bank money triggered a spate of financial sector innovations. The central bank could offer notes with little risk regarding liquidity and public acceptance. On the other hand, notes were costly to use – an example is the considerable interest payments forgone when large amounts are held in cash. With the monetary system firmly anchored, private participants could offer more cost-effective payment solutions: deposit accounts, giro transfers, clearing, and cheques. This system rested on confidence in central bank money. (Stephen F. Quinn and William Roberds (2005), "The Big Problem of Large Bills, the Bank of Amsterdam and the Origins of Central Banking," Federal Reserve Bank of Atlanta Working Paper, 2005–16.)

central bank is nevertheless the fundament of a vast and complex payment system.[24]

The Central Bank

History has shown that monarchs are not always to be trusted to safeguard the monetary system.[25] An institutional solution is to delegate the task of issuing money to

---

[24] Large-value payments between banks are settled continuously in Norges Bank. See Marie N. Lerbak (2013), "Om pengemengden (On the money supply)," Norges Bank Staff Memo No. 14.

[25] A characteristic of money as a means of payment is its anonymous nature. Before the use of money became common among ordinary people, payments usually took place in connection with commercial transactions, whether for goods or services, via networks from which it might be difficult to extricate oneself. The farmer was usually indebted to a town merchant, which resulted in dependency and an obligation to deliver a portion of his produce. Laborers might receive partial payment for their efforts in kind, or at large mills, in scrip that could only be used for purchases in the company store. The monetization of the economy, based on secure monetary values, severed many of these ties of dependency. With money in their pockets, accepted as legal tender everywhere, the farmer or laborer was able to choose. This is also freedom. Nor did the party receiving payment, e.g., the town merchants, have to know more about the customer than that he had money in his pocket and could pay for the goods.

a central bank and shield it from the authorities' temptation to focus on short-term interests.[26]

In Norway, the aim of shielding the monetary system from the government was already embodied in the

[26] A central bank requires mechanisms that ensure confidence. Kydland and Prescott demonstrated that policy makers who tried to pursue an optimal plan for economic policy may have a strong incentive to deviate from the same plan at a later point in time. This will be the case even in the absence of news that would warrant a change in the plan (see F. E. Kydland and E. C. Prescott (1977), "Rules Rather Than Discretion: The Inconsistency of Optimal Plans," *Journal of Political Economy*, Vol. 85, No. 3, pp. 473–491).

The expression "tying oneself to the mast" encapsulates in a simple way how the central bank can avoid the dilemma that Kydland and Prescott describe. The traditional task of the central bank was to issue notes and coins and ensure a well-functioning payment system. But the payment system is only well-functioning when the public has confidence in the value of money. Thus, the primary duty of central banks is to ensure that the value of money is stable. The value of money relies on the confidence of the public that a responsible policy is being pursued. If a central bank is to keep its promise and deliver stable money, it is important that the political authorities stand behind it. Otherwise the central bank will be unable to keep its promise.Throughout history, central banks have tried various mechanisms for tying themselves to the mast. Being accountable for their promises in the form of reporting and follow-up is one mechanism that ensures that the central bank is tied to the mast. Relinquishing the opportunity to break a promise makes that promise more credible. These are matters I touched on in my

Constitution of Norway adopted on 17 May 1814. The drafters of the constitution formulated the following in Article 75(c): "It devolves upon the Storting ... to supervise the monetary affairs of the Realm."

> lecture "On Keeping Promises" in 2008. Keeping a promise is difficult, because reneging on a promise will often be the tempting or rational choice in the short term. The legal scholar and economist Michael Woodford has pointed out that in order to keep your word it is not enough to make a promise today and keep your word tomorrow. When making interest rate forecasts, we must also take into consideration the promises made yesterday. Only then can we fully use expectations to stabilize the economy optimally. This is referred to as monetary policy from a timeless perspective (Michael Woodford (2003), *Interest and Prices*, Princeton University Press). Today there is general consensus that price stability is the best contribution that monetary policy can make to economic stability over time. In the long term, a stable value of money is the only promise that the central bank has the means to deliver. This promise was previously kept by regulating the supply of money issued. Today, the interest rate is the instrument. The central bank does not manage real wages, the labor supply, employment, or the level of unemployment in the long run. But, if price stability is firmly anchored, the central bank can help to reduce short-term economic fluctuations. While central bank independence promotes price stability, researchers do not find a discernible connection between central bank independence and real economic variables such as GDP growth or unemployment (see A. Alesina and L. H. Summers (1993), "Central Bank Independence and Macroeconomic Performance: Some Comparative Evidence," *Journal of Money, Credit and Banking*, Vol. 25, No. 2., pp. 151–162).

This provision strongly censured the Danish King's monetary policy during wartime. In future, representatives appointed by citizens, not the Crown, were to have final responsibility for the monetary system.[27] The king's scope for taxation by means of inflation was curtailed.

The Storting, which was supposed to meet every third year, was not equipped to assume day-to-day responsibility for the monetary system. "Someone" had to do this on behalf of the Storting. That "someone" became Norges Bank, which was established in 1816. The Storting realized that the objectives of monetary policy could be best achieved if the monetary system was shielded from the arbitrary intervention of the monarchy. The distance between the seat of government in Oslo and the central bank in Trondheim was a perhaps deliberate twelve-day journey.[28]

[27] The principle whereby the new state would have its own monetary system, separate from Sweden, was written into the November Constitution in the same year. Here the word "bank" is also used for the first time. In line with the emerging liberal thinking of the time, keeping the value of money secure was considered essential, a prerequisite for the liberty of the citizenry.

[28] This journey time is for transport with a military escort. A post rider was able to make the journey considerably faster. Only after confidence in the new institution had been established – several generations later – was the Bank moved to the capital Christiania. Incidentally, the desire to compensate for the loss of the Bank

At irregular intervals during the past 200 years, Norges Bank has faced *defining moments* – crossroads – that have defined the bank as an institution. At such defining moments, the central bank becomes what it is, both in its own awareness and in that of the general public. These are situations where it sometimes became bigger than itself, or inversely, where it became smaller than itself and did not fulfil its role. As is so often the case, it is only in retrospect that we can fully identify the defining moments and assess the wisdom of the choices made.

Norges Bank faced its first defining moment early on. When it was first established, the Bank was unknown to the public at large. The new paper money, speciedaler notes, was linked by law to a specific amount of silver.[29] Despite the fact that the silver tax had secured Norges Bank a considerable silver reserve, the authorities were

was one of the reasons that Trondheim was chosen as the location for another institution, the Norwegian Institute of Technology.

[29] This was not the first time the Norwegian authorities established a silver standard. In accordance with the regulation of King Haakon V of 1314, silver was to have a standard of purity of 13.5 *lødig*, which is equivalent to a fineness of 844 silver according to the modern method for calculating fineness (Widar Halén (2009), "Arvesølvet og Peter Wessel Zapffes sølvgave (The family silver and Peter Wessel Zapffe's gift of silver)," lecture at the Norwegian Academy of Science and Letters).

afraid to permit free silver redemption. The fear was that the silver fund would be emptied quickly. The notes in circulation with the promise of silver redemption far exceeded the silver value of the silver forks and silver plates that had been collected.

Confidence in the new notes waned, and in 1822 the Storting adopted a long-term strategy whereby the redemption rate in silver for the speciedaler would gradually be increased. The aim – the right to full silver redemption, that is, that the same amount of silver would be paid out as stated on the face of the note – was first achieved twenty years later. I will call this period the *long promise*. The fulfilment of this long promise strengthened and consolidated the Bank's reputation. Perhaps the strongest proof of increased confidence in the central bank was the domination of trade by notes following the introduction of free silver redemption.[30]

The remainder of the nineteenth century until World War I became the heyday of safe money. Inflation was stable throughout, and the Bank kept its promise to redeem its own notes, first in silver and, from 1874, in gold.

Toward the end of the nineteenth century, optimism gained the upper hand in Norway. Increased exports and

---

[30] The speciedaler became legal tender shortly after Norges Bank was established.

strong growth in manufacturing culminated in a wave of speculation in securities and property. In particular, the capital experienced a surge in economic growth and population, which resulted in the construction of large parts of the city as we know it today. The bubble burst in 1899. Under the leadership of the Governor[31] Karl Bomhoff, Norges Bank acted resolutely.[32] For the first time, the Bank acted directly as a lender of last resort for banks to avert a banking crisis. Norges Bank provided

---

[31] Adam Posen, a former member of the Monetary Policy Committee of the Bank of England, compares central banks to pharmacists: "[W]ith a limited medicine cabinet, and restricted by law from exceeding certain bounds, both must make sense of scrawled prescriptions from differing specialists, decide what side effects to take into account, and then ultimately dispense the proper dosage of medicine to their customers, all without knowing or controlling everything else the patient is consuming." See *Foreign Affairs*: www.foreignaffairs.com/articles/139465/adam-s-posen/the-myth-of-the-omnipotent-central-banker.

[32] Karl Bomhoff was appointed as the first Governor of Norges Bank in 1893. By education he was a pharmacist. When Norges Bank's head office was moved to Oslo, Bomhoff also moved to the head office, where there was more extensive expertise than earlier. This facilitated Norges Bank's role as bankers' bank. The theme of my speech is institutions. It might seem paradoxical to refer to physical persons, such as Bomhoff, and not decision-making bodies. However, there is a connection between "what is a central bank" and "who is the central banker."

liquidity to troubled banks, thereby helping to ensure the orderly winding-up of the speculative banks that had sprung up.

Bomhoff's decision in 1899 was a defining moment for Norges Bank, which has since played an important role in dealing with a number of crises as bankers' bank.

After World War I, inflation and large-scale imports of goods caused a loss of confidence in the krone, which dropped considerably in value. When Nicolai Rygg became Governor of Norges Bank in 1920, he started work on putting the monetary system in order. In his view, the central bank was obliged to bring the gold value of the krone back to its prewar level – referred to as *par policy*.[33] However, this ambitious aim entailed years of

---

[33] Also the other Scandinavian countries and the United Kingdom embarked on a similar policy to reintroduce gold convertibility. However, there was a crucial difference. While the Swedish krona had depreciated marginally and sterling by only 10 percent, the Norwegian krone had depreciated by 50 percent in terms of gold. In other words, a substantially tighter policy was necessary compared with those of Sweden and the United Kingdom. It is also an open question whether returning the krone to gold parity after such a steep depreciation actually was in keeping with the orthodox understanding of the gold standard. During the great British debate on the gold peg after the Napoleonic Wars, even David Ricardo, the gold standard's most ardent defender, warned against returning to earlier parity values after a sharp depreciation. Milton

strong deflation and blight before the gold value was achieved in 1928.

For ninety years, historians have discussed par policy. My contribution will have to be a present-time analysis with the inherent scope and limitations.[34] Was this a good policy? There is no doubt that the motives were good. Rygg considered that Norges Bank had a moral obligation to keep its word, as it had done a century earlier, but was also of the view that this was rational in the longer term. There is also no doubt that Rygg adhered to the rules of the game. Par policy had the support of the political authorities. Nevertheless, an action must also be assessed by the outcome. The central bank was blinded by the old gold content as a guideline for monetary policy and implemented a policy that inflicted large-scale real economic costs on the country. Many countries had suspended the gold standard during the war, but no other

Friedman and Anna Jacobson Schwartz (1963), *A Monetary History of the United States of America, 1867–1960*, National Bureau of Economic Research, p. 82.

[34] Since the past is our laboratory and the source from which we draw lessons, it is more fruitful to try to understand the past on its own terms than to sit in judgment over it. Anything else would make history as a serious branch of study into a meaningless exercise, reducing it to a running, constantly changing contemporary commentary on what has been.

country pursued such an ambitious par policy in the 1920s.[35] Norges Bank was deaf to growing contemporary criticism and sustained a substantial reputational loss.[36] As a consequence, the Bank's ability to fulfill its role in society was weakened for decades to come.

The par policy failure was an important reason behind the postwar opposition to allowing the central bank to make monetary policy decisions independently.[37]

---

[35] In the opinion piece "Mytedannelsen om paripolitikken (Myth-making and par policy)," Hermod Skånland points to the strong political support for par policy in the 1920s and to the fact that growth was higher in Norway than in its neighboring countries: "Against this background, it might be difficult to understand that par policy has endured as the great policy blunder of the 1920s, and Rygg as the primary culprit for the ills that followed.... This had to do with the fact that the flexibility that could be obtained through monetary policy was more to the liking of leading economists in the 1930s and up to the present day, than the stability and the long-termism that may result when one imposes constraints on oneself of the type Nicolai Rygg represented." See *Aftenposten*, 30 May 1998.

[36] The Bank *must* on occasion be deaf to contemporary criticism in order to safeguard long-term considerations. But there will be a trade-off: which short-term costs are we willing to bear to keep our long-term promises.

[37] www.norges-bank.no/Upload/67282/Artikkel_Gjedrem_180408.pdf.

A prominent feature of the postwar period was the conviction that the economy could be micromanaged by coordinating instruments drawn up by the government. At the time, few people considered this state of affairs as problematic. Although inflation was higher than before, unemployment was low and growth strong. This approach was in line with the dominant philosophy abroad, although the Norwegian variant was probably taken a step further than in most other countries.

The then-governor of Norges Bank, Erik Brofoss, had both time and energy to concentrate on matters that interested him but which differed from the traditional interests of a central bank. Brofoss was, for example, keen to solve the housing shortage problem following the war. He had visited England and been inspired by the New Towns.[38] He asked the Bank's lawyers to draft a Norwegian statutory bill based on the British act of 1946.

Norges Bank Governor Knut Getz Wold was even clearer about the Bank's reduced role in monetary policy. In a speech in 1972, he stated the following:

---

[38] In a letter to Norway's ambassador in London dated 1963, for example, he wrote: "As you may have seen from the Norwegian newspapers, I have in several lectures proposed that we should consider building entirely new towns as part of solving the problems of the districts." Discussions with Viking Medstad on 3 January and 24 October 2013.

Cartels and price agreements play an increasing role in the setting of prices. The social partners exercise decisive influence over wage developments. Agricultural prices are set in negotiations between the agricultural organisations and the state.... In these circumstances, it is almost meaningless to talk about the central bank's special responsibility for inflation.[39]

The diminished role of the institution, which persisted well into the 1980s, must be seen in the light of mixed experiences with par policy, ambitious aims of micromanaging the economy, and the conviction that lower unemployment could be achieved by accepting higher inflation.[40] At the same time, major imbalances were building up in the economy. Fiscal policy, in conjunction with credit regulation and tight political control of business investment, gradually undermined the monetary system as an institution. Later in the 1970s, these problems came to the surface. Growth declined, inflation surged, and unemployment rose sharply. I should add that these problems were not confined to Norway. In

[39] www.nhh.no/Files/Filer/Om%20NHH/lehmkuhlforelesning/lehm kuhl 1972.pdf

[40] Thomas N. Berg (2011), "Mellom politikk og marked (Between policy and market)," Norges Bank Staff Memo No. 19, Norges Bank, www.norges-bank.no/Upload/Publikasjoner/Staff%20Memo/2011/StaffMemo_1911.pdf, p. 62.

1971 the Bretton Woods system collapsed. Two years later the first oil price shock occurred.

At the beginning of the 1980s, the problems in the Norwegian economy had reached a pinnacle. In May 1986, the Brundtland government decided to devalue the Norwegian krone by 10 percent. As was usual on such occasions, it was said that this would be the "last time." Less usual was that it actually was the last time. Prime Minister Gro Harlem Brundtland, Minister of Finance Gunnar Berge, and State Secretary Bjørn Skogstad Aamo had come to a decision. Devaluation policy was consigned to the past. Price stability, defined as low and stable inflation in line with that of trading partners, was established as an anchor for economic policy.[41] To implement this policy, both the monetary system and Norges Bank had to be reestablished as independent institutions.

Whether the government gave or Norges Bank repossessed control over the policy instruments, especially the key policy rate, remains subject to debate. But the result was that Norges Bank in fact gained independence

---

[41] In autumn 1987, Gro Harlem Brundtland and Gunnar Berge had to defend Norges Bank's independence in interest rate setting to fellow party members, members of the Storting and the central committee during what was called the "interest rate uproar." Frank Rossavik (2007), *Stikk i strid. Ein biografi om Einar Førde [At variance. A biography of Einar Førde]*, Oslo: Spartacus.

in interest rate setting to achieve the government-defined policy objectives. Inflation fell from double-digit figures around 1980 to 2–3 percent a decade later.

During the banking crisis around 1990, Norges Bank played a key role, which Bomhoff had paved the way for ninety years earlier, as a provider of liquidity to troubled banks.

During the 1990s, the intellectual basis for modern monetary policy was laid in Norges Bank. The transition from exchange rate targeting to inflation targeting, with an explicit price stability objective, occurred gradually, and was formally introduced in March 2001. A new order was established. Norges Bank was again responsible for the monetary system. The institution was reconstituted.

The defining moments in both the initial and latter period of Norges Bank's 200-year evolution were thus quite long. I called the period 1822 to1842 the *long promise*. The period 1986 to 2001 can be described as the *long return*.

But we must not allow complacency to set in. The world economy is still marked by the financial crisis that took hold in 2008. This is the first major crisis to hit the West's monetary system since the gold standard was abandoned in 1971.[42] In addressing the crisis, many

[42] Philip Coggan (2012), *Paper Promises: Debt, Money and the New World Order*, London: Penguin.

central banks have deployed unconventional instruments. Both the Federal Reserve and the Bank of England have lent substantial amounts of money and implemented unorthodox measures. Central bank governors might feel that they have recently faced many defining moments in a short time span. Many might say that they have drawn on the institutions' accumulated confidence. Only time will tell whether these defining moments have truly secured the monetary system and central bank independence.

Conclusion

Public institutions are the product of their tasks and history. The monetary system was shaken when Norges Bank solely focused on bringing the krone's value back to par. We might say that the institution lost sight of broader social responsibilities. But the monetary system also suffered in the following period when the authorities took control and lost sight of the central bank. The conclusion with regard to the monetary system is that it must be both steered and guarded. The political authorities must define the objectives and the central bank must be the devoted guardian of the monetary system. The central bank must deliver price stability, a robust payment system, and a stable financial system.

On Central Banking

It is in its performance of this responsibility that the central bank contributes to realizing the mandate issued by the Storting – to supervise the monetary system.

Inspired by the former Governor of the Bank of England, Mervyn King, I will summarize my experiences in a few *simple* principles, which, if followed, would enable institutions to fulfil their role in society and serve its citizens:[43]

1. It must know its social responsibility and restrict itself to the pursuit of the defined objectives and not be distracted by extraneous concerns – it must keep its promises.
2. It must use its instruments and expertise to achieve the objectives – it must make good decisions.
3. Leaders must be aware that the institution will be held accountable – it must practice transparency as a principle.

---

[43] Many attempt to measure whether institutions are fulfilling their societal role, which is a difficult exercise. As a nation, Norway scores high. Individual institutions are also measured. If any of us has preconceived notions, at least mine bear out. The institutions I thought would be at the bottom of such lists are at the bottom, and vice versa – those I thought would be at the top are at the top. But this is not a static situation. Movement is possible – in both directions.

4. Leaders must utilize institutional memory and staff experience – they must learn from history and manage their wealth – their cultural heritage.

These principles also summarize the six speeches I have given at the Academy of Science and Letters: a good institution keeps promises, makes good decisions, practices transparency as a governance principle, learns from its own history, and manages its cultural heritage.

And the threads are gathered here. Today's speech seeks to encompass all the themes in one frame. The lessons learned from Norges Bank's first 200 years and the criteria I just cited are useful both in Norges Bank's daily work and in making longer-term assessments. I would argue that these general principles apply to other institutions too, whether legal, cultural, or educational. Decisions that are made in these institutions determine whether a country's citizens can live a life of freedom and prosperity.

Index

Index

Index

Index

Index

Index

Index

Index

Index

Index

politics
economic policy and, 140–141
independent decision making and,
69–70
market liberalisation and, 36–38
voting rights in companies and,
118–121
Posen, Adam, 179n.31
premise-based decision making,
86–89
Prescott, Edward, xiii–xv, 1–5, 22,
174–175n.26
price indexes
inflation targeting and, 24–29
scraping technology and analysis
of, 170–171n.21
price stability, 10–13
central bank promise of, 23–24,
28–29, 174–175n.26
economic policy linked to, 185–187
historical perspectives on,
130–132
inflation targeting and, 17–20,
24–29, 185–187
monetary institutions and,
167–171
monetary policy and, 22–29,
89–93
scraping technology for pricing
data and, 170–171n.21
PriceStats, 170–171n.21
Primary School Act, 164–165
promises of central banks
commitment to, xiii–xv
difficulty of keeping, 1–5
timeless perspective in, 28–29,
174–175n.26
property rights, economic growth
and, 158n.3

Public Administration Act of 1967
(Norway), 36–38
public expenditure, oil revenue
funding of, 104–106

Quinn, Stephen, 172n.23

real capital, wealth management and,
104–106
real estate, wealth management and,
117–118
regulatory regimes
business cycles and fluctuations in,
147–149
economic crises and, 36–38
historical perspectives on, 133–137
pendulum swings and, 138n.13
Reinhart, Carmen, 140
relativity, theory of, 126–128n.2
rent-seeking, resource curse and,
106–107
resource curse
institutions and, 158–159n.4
wealth management, 106–107
"return-free risk" principle, 117–118
return maximisation, wealth
management and, 114–118
Rigobon, Roberto, 170–171n.21
risk-return tradeoff, wealth
management and, 113
Robinson, J., xxii–xxiv, 159–162
Rogoff, Kenneth, 140
Rule of Four, xx–xxii
Rygg, Nicolai, xiii–xv, xxii–xxiv,
128–129, 139–140n.14, 180–181

Sachs, Gunter, 106, 121–123
Sachs, Jeffrey, 106–107, 159n.5
Schelling, Thomas, xiii–xv, 1–5

Index

Index

Printed in the United States
By Bookmasters